LARGE-SCALE ASSESSMENT ISSUES AND PRACTICES AN INTRODUCTORY HANDBOOK

Printed in the United States of America
Lightning Source (Ingram) Books Inc.
1246 Heil Quaker Blvd.
La Vergne, TN 37086
USA

Printed in the United Kingdom
Lightning Source (Ingram) Books Ltd.
Chapter House
Pitfield, Kiln Farm
Milton Keynes MK 11 3LW
UK

Printed in Australia
Lightning Source (Ingram) Books Ltd.
Unit A 1/A3
7 Janine Street
Scoresby, Victoria 3179
Australia

Cover, Design, Page Layout and Composition
Lidija Markovic

Canadian Cataloguing in Publication Data
Jones, Richard Merrick, 1947-

Large-Scale Assessment Issues and Practices:
An Introductory Handbook
ISBN: 978-0-9684857-3-6
1. Assessment   2. Testing   3. Large-Scale
4. Jones, Richard Merrick

© Copyright Richard Merrick Jones, 2014

ALL RIGHTS RESERVED
No part of this book may be reproduced in any form without the written permission of the author.

LARGE-SCALE ASSESSMENT ISSUES AND PRACTICES

AN INTRODUCTORY HANDBOOK

RICHARD M. JONES

CONTENTS

Acknowledgements VI
About the Author VII

1 INTRODUCTION

Education Reform and
Large-Scale Assessment 1
Best-Of-Class Assessments 4
Purposes of the Handbook 5
Organization of the Handbook 6

2 FOUNDATIONS

Introduction 7
Framework Document 8
Summary 26

3 ITEM DEVELOPMENT

Ethical Considerations 27
Test Design 28
Test Development Approaches 30
Assessment Blueprint 32
Item Development 38
Summary 62

4 FIELD TESTING AND ITEM SELECTION

Field Testing Multiple-Choice and Open-Response Items that Require a Short Response 63
Open-Response Items that Require an Extended Response 65
Item Selection of Multiple-Choice and Open-Response Items that Require a Short Response 67
Test Form Construction 76
Item Banking 79
Questionnaires 79
Summary 82

5 TEST ADMINISTRATION

Ethical Considerations 83
Administration Guides 85
Accommodations 86
Deferrals and Exemptions 86
Accommodations Guides 87
Other Supportive Documents and Resources 89
Administration Schedule 90
Distribution and Receipt of Assessment Materials 91
Administration Formats 92
Quality Assurance in Test Administration 92
Appeals 95
Summary 96

OPEN-RESPONSE SCORING

Ethical Considerations   97
Approaches to Scoring   98
EQAO Scoring Process   100
Summary   118

STANDARD SETTING

Ethical Considerations   119
Common Standard-Setting Methods   120
Typical Standard-Setting Steps   125
Cross-Grade Standard Setting   130
EQAO's Approach to Standard Setting   131
Summary   136

DATA INTEGRITY, ANALYSIS AND EQUATING

Ethical Considerations   137
Equating Designs   141
Statistical Approaches to Equating   142
The EQAO Approach to Equating   146
Summary   148

REPORTING AND USE OF DATA/RESULTS

Ethical Considerations   149
Level of Reporting   150
Content and Nature of Reports   151
Interpretive Frames   151
Need to Maintain Confidentiality   153
Appeal Process   153
Technical Report   154
EQAO's Approach to Reporting   154
Outreach   163
Research   164
Summary   166

ALTERNATE ASSESSMENTS

Ethical Considerations   167
Approaches to Alternate Assessment   168
Scoring Alternate Assessments   169
Ontario's Approach to Alternate Assessment   170
Summary   174

CONCLUSION   175

Glossary   177
Appendix: Principles for Fair Student Assessment Practices for Education in Canada (1993)   **188**
References   209

ACKNOWLEDGEMENTS

Many people contributed in a variety of ways to the preparation of this handbook.

First of all, I wish to express my appreciation to the Joint Advisory Committee, through the Chair, for granting me permission to include the document *Principles for Fair Student Assessment Practices for Education in Canada* (1993) in this publication.

Dr. Barbara Plake, Professor Emeritus, University of Nebraska-Lincoln and Dr. Mark Reckase, Professor Emeritus, Michigan State University reviewed and provided insightful comments on the standard-setting and equating chapters, respectively.

Ally Feng, psychometrician, Curriculum and Assessment Branch, British Columbia Ministry of Education and Dr. Ping Yang, Manager of Scoring and Reporting, Alberta Education supplied valuable information about their respective provincial assessment programs, particularly the equating of test results.

Many of my colleagues at the Education Quality and Accountability Office (EQAO) gave generously of their time and expertise to provide advice and comments on drafts of the entire manuscript or portions of it. In particular, I would like to acknowledge the contributions of Dr. Michael Kozlow, former Director of Data and Support Services; Dr. Nizam Radwan, Psychometrician; Joanne Rinella, Program Manager, Secondary Assessments; Lisa Amati, Program Manager, Elementary Assessments; and Angela Hinton, Acting Director of Data and Support Services who, in addition to reviewing the complete manuscript, contributed the section on ensuring data integrity in Chapter 8.

Lidija Markovic's expertise and creativity in document design, page layout and composition contributed much to the successful completion of this project.

I am grateful to Bruce Rodrigues, Chief Executive Officer and Debra Rantz, Chief Assessment Officer of EQAO for their support of my publishing this handbook and for granting me permission to use and/or adapt agency assessment-related documents and materials.

A special note of appreciation is extended to Dr. Todd Rogers, Professor Emeritus, University of Alberta, for his expert advice and editing suggestions during the writing of this handbook.

ABOUT THE AUTHOR

Richard Jones has worked in the field of large-scale student assessment for nearly three decades. Currently, he is Director of Assessment and Reporting with the Education Quality and Accountability Office (EQAO) in Toronto.[1] Prior to his current position, Dr. Jones was Project Manager for National, International and Special Projects with EQAO; Director of Assessment and Evaluation with the Saskatchewan Department of Education; and Coordinator of Provincial Learning Assessment and Assistant Director of the Provincial and Scholarship Examination Program with the British Columbia Ministry of Education. In these various roles his responsibilities included designing and implementing initiatives related to student evaluation, program evaluation, curriculum evaluation, provincial learning assessment, education quality indicators, school and school board improvement planning and accreditation, as well as national and international student assessments.

Prior to working in the field of assessment and evaluation, Dr. Jones served as researcher and senior manager for an American-based consulting firm on projects based in the Middle East. He has several years of teaching experience at elementary, secondary, community college and university levels in Canada and Africa. Over the years, he has consulted, made presentations at conferences and authored numerous journal articles and book chapters on assessment and evaluation topics.

---

[1] *EQAO is an arms-length, independent agency of the Ontario Government, established through the Education Quality and Accountability Office Act (1996) in response to recommendations from the 1994 Royal Commission on Learning. The agency is responsible for the development, administration scoring and reporting of Ontario's provincial large-scale assessment program and coordinates the province's involvement in national and international assessments. More information about EQAO is available on the agency's Web site at www.eqao.com.*

CHAPTER ONE

INTRODUCTION

EDUCATION REFORM AND LARGE-SCALE ASSESSMENT

Over the past three decades jurisdictions have established a variety of education reform initiatives in response to the need for provincial, state and national public accountability in elementary and secondary schools and for improvement of their education systems. As part of education reform, many jurisdictions have established large-scale assessment programs that often include learning assessment programs that measure the academic progress of students in various subjects at key stages in their elementary and/or secondary school careers and/or high-stakes secondary school exit examinations. There has been a proliferation of large-scale assessment programs across Canada, the United States and around the world.

The Council of Ministers of Education, Canada (CMEC) (2013) explains that because in Canada there is no national department/ministry of education, education falls under provincial or territorial jurisdiction. Consequently, each province and territory is responsible for the development of the curriculum and the program of large-scale student assessment within its jurisdiction. Surveys conducted by Volante (2006) and Klinger, DeLuca and Miller (2008) show that every Canadian province and territory has some form of large-scale assessment of student achievement. Testing is administered at various grade levels and in different subjects, commonly including the core subjects of literacy (reading and writing) and mathematics. In addition to provincial and territorial assessment programs, the Canadian provinces/territories participate in the CMEC-coordinated Pan-Canadian Assessment Program (PCAP), which assesses the performance of Grade 8 students in reading, mathematics and science. Some provinces/territories also participate in international assessments such as the Program for International Student Assessment (PISA), administered by the Organisation for Economic Co-operation and Development (OECD), to assess the reading, mathematics and science knowledge and skills of 15-year-old students; the Progress in International Reading Literacy Study (PIRLS), conducted under the auspices of the International Association for the Evaluation of Educational Achievement (IEA), to assess 9-year-old students' reading literacy; and the Trends in International Mathematics and Science Study (TIMSS), also conducted under the auspices of the (IEA), to assess the mathematics and science knowledge and skills of 9- and 13-year-old students.

In the United States, tests administered by state and national education departments have been a long-time cornerstone of education systems. The National Assessment of Educational Progress (NAEP), administered by the National Center for Education Statistics within the U.S. Department of Education, has been conducting national/state assessments of students in Grades 4, 8 and 12 in a variety of subjects for many years. Tests are most frequently administered in reading, writing, mathematics and science, while other subjects such as the arts, civics, economics, geography and U.S. history are assessed periodically. Technology and Engineering Literacy assessments were planned to begin in 2014. Recognizing that the school system was not providing the skills and knowledge high-school graduates need to be adequately prepared for post-secondary education or the world of work, the National Governors Association, in cooperation with the Council of Chief State School Officers, initiated development of new Common Core State Standards (Common Core State Standards Initiative, 2014). The standards (curriculum learning expectations) for mathematics and English language arts were released in 2010. Two consortiums: the Partnership for Assessment of Readiness for College and Careers (PARCC) and Smarter Balanced, each with their respective member states, were established with different approaches to assessing the standards. According to the PARCC and Smarter Balanced consortiums (2013), assessment of the Common Core State Standards is expected to begin in 2014-2015.

Beyond the North American context, several authors/organizations, including the Education, Audiovisual and Culture Executive Agency (2009), Greaney and Kellaghan (2008) and Takayama (2013), describe education reform initiatives, including large-scale assessment programs in Africa, Asia, Australia, New Zealand, Europe and South America. Large-scale assessment is truly a worldwide phenomenon.

Large-scale assessment programs take many forms and purport to serve a variety of purposes. For instance, some programs rely on closed-response items/questions (sometimes referred to as selected-response items, which include multiple-choice), open-response items (sometimes called written- or constructed-response) or performance item formats, while others contain a blend of item types. Some programs are designed to gauge the extent to which students have attained curricular learning objectives for public accountability and improvement purposes (referred to here as provincial/state/national learning assessments). Others are designed to certify that students have attained the knowledge and skills to graduate from high school (referred to here as secondary school exit examinations).

BEST-OF-CLASS ASSESSMENTS

For many years, EQAO, the organization of which I am the Director of Assessment and Reporting, has conducted Primary Division (Grade 3) and the Junior Division (Grade 6) assessments of reading, writing and mathematics; a Grade 9 mathematics assessment in Academic and in Applied Mathematics; and a Grade 10 reading and writing assessment called the Ontario Secondary School Literacy Test (OSSLT) in Canada's two official languages. All of these assessments are administered annually.

Following several years of assessments, EQAO launched a comprehensive review of all aspects of its assessment program. This process involved an extensive review by external national and international assessment experts, consultation with the province's educator and stakeholder groups, representatives of the commercial testing industry and consideration of research on best practices in large-scale testing around the world. All of the information gathered from the review was given careful consideration in the re-design of EQAO's assessment programs. The booklet *Ensuring Quality Assessments: Enhancements to EQAO's Assessment Program: The Move Forward* (2004) provides an overview of the review process and the suggested enhancements to Ontario's assessment program and appears in the list of references at the end of this handbook.

In each chapter of this resource, EQAO assessment practices are described following general discussion of issues. EQAO's practices are highlighted because the agency has been recognized for its high-quality assessments. In its 2009 audit of EQAO, the Office of the Auditor General of Ontario found the agency's procedures and controls ensured that the provincial assessments accurately reflected the Ministry of Education's curriculum expectations. Another audit, conducted by Fremer (2011) concluded that

> ...EQAO has established sound, world-class quality assurance procedures for test administration. (p.3)

Furthermore, a review of EQAO assessment quality, conducted by Rogers (2013), states that

> The procedures used to develop and review assessment and questionnaire items, administer the assessments to students, score student responses, analyze and equate the results of the previous and current years, and report the results and ensure they are used are best of class procedures. EQAO's quality assurance procedures are equally compelling, as is its willingness to examine its own procedures to ensure that the ones in use are current and best of class. (p.49)

Many of the best practices, shared in this handbook, are excerpted or adapted from various EQAO documents, including the agency's technical reports of the assessments, which may be accessed at www.eqao.com.

PURPOSES OF THE HANDBOOK

Over the course of nearly 30 years, I have served in three Canadian provinces as a coordinator and senior manager of large-scale testing programs. Personal experiences from these assessment programs are also shared here. Although each program addressed unique challenges, many testing issues have been, and remain, common.

This handbook focuses on common issues in large-scale assessments and provides practical information and advice (based on experience, research and best practices) to support their effective design, development and implementation. It is meant to be a resource for those who wish to establish or enhance large-scale assessment programs, as well as for students of introductory post-secondary courses on large-scale assessment. It is hoped that the information in this handbook will provide a springboard for more in-depth study of the topics introduced here.

Sometimes, distinctions are made between the terms *testing* and *assessment*. Whereas *testing* may refer to the administration of a single measurement instrument or set of instruments, *assessment* may be used to describe the collection of data and information using multiple methods, including tests. For the purposes of this handbook, however, the two terms are used interchangeably.

ORGANIZATION OF THE HANDBOOK

This resource is organized sequentially, beginning with foundational issues and decisions that need to be addressed prior to designing, developing and implementing a large-scale assessment program. Other general topics, including test design and item development, administration, scoring, data analysis and reporting are presented in the sequence of the traditional testing cycle. Since ethics in large-scale assessment is a major focus of this handbook, the document *Principles for Fair Student Assessment Practices for Education in Canada* (1993) is presented in its entirety in the Appendix. Part B of the *Principles* document deals with large-scale assessments (assessments produced external to the classroom). A glossary of terms and selected references are also provided at the end of this handbook.

CHAPTER TWO

FOUNDATIONS

INTRODUCTION

There are many issues to consider and decisions that must be made before embarking on the design and development of a large-scale testing program. If timing and other circumstances permit, it is useful to involve key stakeholder groups in these discussions, as this will increase the likelihood that the program will have the benefit of input from a variety of sources and enjoy as much support as possible.

As decisions about important fundamental principles of the assessment program are made, it is useful to record them in a document referred to here as a framework document. This type of foundational document provides a critically important resource for staff involved in program design, development and implementation. In addition, if it is made publicly available, the document will demonstrate transparency, which will contribute to the promotion of wider understanding and acceptance of the program.

FRAMEWORK DOCUMENT

At a minimum, the framework document should provide information about the purpose(s) of the large-scale assessment program, the main guiding principles underlying the assessment process and how the resulting information will be used and reported. A comprehensive framework document may include the following types of information:

- Ethical considerations
- Purpose(s) of the specific large-scale assessment program
- Frame of reference for interpretation (norm- or criterion-referenced)
- Differences between large-scale and classroom assessments
- Language(s) of testing
- Sample versus census testing
- Definition(s) of the construct(s) that will be measured
- Alignment with provincial/state/national curricula, incorporating current research on assessment in the relevant subject(s)
- Curriculum learning expectations (some jurisdictions refer to these as content standards or learning outcomes) that will and will not be measured
- Content and timing of the test
- Item development
- Field testing
- Accommodations, special provisions, deferrals and exemptions
- Alternate assessments (where applicable)
- Scoring
- Reporting
- Maintaining consistency of administration and over time

Each of these topics is briefly described in this chapter and elaborated in subsequent ones.

Ethical Considerations

Since humans are involved in the design, development, administration, scoring and reporting of large-scale assessments, a significant amount of subjective, professional judgement comes into play. In order to ensure fairness and equity, the assessment program should subscribe to key principles that can be referred to during all phases of an assessment program. For instance, one important principle in creating test items for large-scale assessment is that developers should make them as fair as possible for students from all backgrounds, including those of different cultures, genders and geographic regions, as well students with special learning needs. Statements about these fundamental principles should be referenced in the framework document. In Canada, the *Principles for Fair Student Assessment Practices for Education in Canada* (1993) (included in the Appendix of this handbook) provides principles and related guidelines that are generally accepted by a wide range of education- and assessment-related organizations. In the United States there are several similar resources, one of which is the *Standards for Educational and Psychological Testing* (American Educational Research Association, the American Psychological Association & the National Council on Measurement in Education, 1999).

Purpose(s) of Large-Scale Assessments

Large-scale assessment purposes can be many and varied. Following are some possible purposes:

- Provide information for public accountability of the education system at the school, school board, province/state and/or national levels
- Provide information for school and school board improvement planning
- Provide diagnostic information to improve individual student learning (diagnostic tests tend to be lengthy in order to gather sufficient data)
- Examine the extent to which the mandated curriculum is being taught
- Influence classroom curriculum and instruction

- Certify that students have acquired certain levels of competency for promotion or graduation
- Provide information for comparative purposes (schools, school boards, provinces/states, countries) over time

Decisions about the purpose(s) of a large-scale assessment program should be clearly articulated before development work is initiated. The purpose(s) will ultimately drive all aspects of the program and have implications for its design. For instance, if the main goal of one program is public accountability at the school, school board, province/state and/or national level and another's is to provide diagnostic information to improve individual student learning, the assessment programs are likely to differ significantly in a number of respects. For example, if the intention is to report on the relative strengths and weaknesses of individual students in each of the mathematics strands of number sense and numeration, measurement, geometry and spatial sense, patterning and algebra, and data management and probability, then several items need to be developed to cover the range of curriculum learning expectations for each strand. This approach carries a variety of implications including the financial costs associated with development, scoring and reporting, as well as potential disruptions in schools caused by the burden of a relatively large amount of testing time. On the other hand, if the large-scale assessment program's primary purpose is public accountability, a broad sampling of the mathematics curriculum, resulting in overall test scores for students, might be appropriate. In addition, a random sample of schools and students could also be used for this purpose, rather than involving the entire cohort of students, thus resulting in lower financial and other costs. Both approaches require sufficient numbers of items to ensure valid and reliable reporting.

Assessment programs should be developed to address a small number of clearly stated purposes; it is difficult, if not impossible, to design an assessment that effectively addresses multiple purposes. Among other things, the review of EQAO's assessment program (Wolfe, Childs, & Elgie, 2004) found that the assessments were expected to serve a "myriad" of purposes, and a recommendation was made to clarify them and include statements about the relative importance of each. Examples of purpose statements for each of EQAO's large-scale assessments can be found in the framework documents for the Primary Division (Grades 1-3) and Junior Division (Grades 4-6) Reading, Writing and Mathematics; Grade 9 Mathematics and Ontario Secondary School Literacy Test (OSSLT) assessments at www.eqao.com.

Frame of Reference for Interpretation (Norm- or Criterion-Referenced)

A decision needs to be made about whether the assessment will be norm- or criterion-referenced. Redfield (2001) defines these terms as follows:

Norm-referenced achievement results or scores are

> referenced (i.e., compared) to a norm, the norm being the range of scores for all students who took the test when it was normed. Many commercial achievement tests have national norms for groups of students at different age or grade levels.

Criterion-referenced achievement results or scores

> are compared to an established criterion or definition/description of performance. The criterion may be a predetermined number of correct responses or, in the case of performance tasks, a response that meets certain criteria for competent performance such as proper use of conventions and logical, supporting ideas for a point of view in writing. (p. 2)

In recent years there has been a general shift away from norm-referenced to a greater emphasis on criterion-referenced tests, as provinces, states and countries have required tests to be designed to reflect specific curriculum learning expectations (content standards or outcomes). More information about reporting is presented in Chapter 9.

Differences Between Large-scale and Classroom Assessment

Student assessment is an essential part of the teaching and learning process. Teachers use assessment in the classroom for formative, summative and diagnostic purposes to gather information about the knowledge and skills that students are acquiring to

- see how the class is doing as a whole and whether learning has taken place;
- adapt instruction as needed;
- identify students in need of remedial help and the nature of that help;
- encourage or foster student learning and
- formulate grades to be included in reporting.

A traditional test is one kind of classroom assessment; however, information about student learning progress is gathered on an ongoing basis and can be collected in a variety of other ways, including quizzes, projects, presentations, portfolios of student work, oral assessments, as well as observation checklists of student behaviours. Large-scale assessments, on the other hand, are usually single-point-in-time tests that measure achievement in given subjects at critical points in students' school careers.

Classroom assessment and large-scale assessment have differing purposes and must conform to different constraints. Table 1 provides some important distinctions between the two types of assessment.

Language(s) of Testing

In some jurisdictions, the large-scale assessment program is developed in only one language. In other jurisdictions, however, there may be a requirement for the testing to be developed and administered in two or more languages. For instance, many U.S. states are required to provide tests in English and Spanish. In Canada, where French and English are the two official languages, most provinces provide tests in both French and English. Developing, administering, scoring and reporting assessments in two or more languages raise numerous questions that must be answered

TABLE 1: Differences Between Large-Scale and Classroom Assessment

LARGE-SCALE ASSESSMENT	CLASSROOM ASSESSMENT
The purpose of many large-scale assessments is to provide comparable year-to-year data to give the public information on student achievement.	The purposes of classroom assessment are to improve student learning, to report regularly on student achievement and to provide timely, constructive feedback for improvement.
Many large-scale assessments provide reliable, objective data that can inform improvement planning and target setting at the class, school and/or province/state/national levels.	Classroom assessments encourage students to engage in self-evaluation and personal goal setting. They also provide parents with information on strengths and weaknesses that can be used to encourage improvement.
Large-scale assessment materials are created and scored "at a distance." The assessment scorers do not know the students personally.	Classroom assessment materials are usually created and marked by a teacher who knows the students personally.
Large-scale assessments are summative; they present a snapshot of student achievement at the time the assessment is administered.	Classroom assessments are conducted in an instructional context and include diagnostic, formative and summative assessment. They are administered at regular intervals over time.
Large-scale assessments require students to demonstrate their knowledge and skills independently on standardized tasks and under standardized conditions, although some accommodations are allowed for students with special education needs.	A wide variety of supports (reminders, clarification) are often available to address students' special education needs and abilities.
Large-scale assessments measure achievement against expectations from the prescribed curriculum and contain tasks and items that sample from and represent the curriculum for the domain assessed.	Classroom assessments measure expectations from the curriculum and contain tasks and items that represent expectations, topics and themes that have been taught. The questions are written in language used regularly in the classroom by the teacher.
Large-scale assessments provide the same (in a given year) or psychometrically comparable items (from year to year) for all students.	Classroom assessments can provide modified items or tasks tailored to the special education needs of individuals or groups of students.
In order for students' results on large-scale assessments to be comparable across the jurisdiction, the assessments must be administered, scored and reported on in a consistent and standardized manner.	Results of classroom assessments across the province are not always comparable, because of the variation in administration procedures and time allowed, amount of teacher support, modification of items to suit student needs and teacher autonomy in marking.
For large-scale assessments, all scorers use the same scoring guides and are trained and monitored to ensure objectivity and consistency.	The marking of classroom assessments is more subjective and is often influenced by contextual information about the students that is available to the teacher.

Source: Adapted from information provided in all EQAO assessment framework documents (2007a, b & c/2009); © by EQAO, used with permission.

and challenges that must be met. For example, there is the question about whether or not the test in one language will be a translation of the other language or whether different tests will be generated independently in each language. (Most jurisdictions translate tests from one language to another/others.) One of many implications of the answer to this question will be the financial cost. A statement about the language(s) of testing should appear in the framework document. In Ontario, an important underlying principle of the EQAO assessment program is that all assessments are offered, in equal quality, in both official languages. Since there are some curricular differences between the French- and English-language school systems, the tests are different and are developed independently in the two languages. Although the content of the tests are different to reflect the different constructs being measured in English and French, their structure (number and types of items, test length, layout/look) is the same.

Sample versus Census Tests

Another important decision that must be made prior to the design of a large-scale assessment and that should be described in the framework document is whether the test will be administered to a sample of students and schools in a jurisdiction, or whether all students (a census) will be involved. This decision has several implications for the assessment's design. For instance, if samples of students and schools are chosen randomly, reporting will most likely be possible only at the provincial/state or national level. Reporting will most likely not be possible at the individual student, school or school board levels. Furthermore, it will be more difficult to link results for cohorts of students from one assessment to the next. Sample tests usually cost the same as census tests to develop, but do not cost as much to administer and score. Some jurisdictions, however, use matrix sampling to increase coverage of the curriculum expectations when assessments are administered to samples of students. This approach can increase the cost of test development because more test items need to be developed, but reporting possibilities may be enhanced. The purpose(s) of the testing program will greatly influence the decision about whether the assessment will involve a census or a sample of students and schools.

Defining the Construct

An early task in developing a large-scale assessment program is to determine the subject matter and the age or grade of the students to be tested. In many jurisdictions these decisions are mandated by provincial/state, national or international authorities. Once these basic decisions are made, the definition of the construct(s) [sometimes referred to as domain(s)] to be measured, as well as connections to the curriculum and current research must be established. For instance, it is important to establish what is meant by the terms such as "literacy," "reading," "writing" and "mathematics." An essential starting point in defining the construct(s) is the associated curriculum; however, curriculum documents do not always provide sufficiently clear definitions upon which to build an assessment design. A good example of this is the concept of literacy, which has been defined in a host of different ways (e.g., functional literacy, information literacy, media literacy, visual literacy, global literacy, technological literacy). Unless there is a clear understanding of the meaning of literacy from the outset, research may need to be conducted (including reference to the constructs used in other provincial/state, national and international testing programs) and decisions made as to what specifically is meant by "literacy" for the purposes of the assessment. The description of literacy in the OSSLT framework document (2007c), available at the EQAO Web site, provides a good example of the type of information required to adequately define a construct for large-scale assessment:

> The purpose of the OSSLT is to determine whether a student has the literacy (reading and writing) skills required to meet the standard for understanding reading selections and communicating in a variety of writing forms expected by *The Ontario Curriculum* across all grades up to the end of Grade 9. (p. 6)

This description of literacy is appropriate for the OSSLT as it is developed and administered today; however, it should be noted that many large-scale assessment programs, including Ontario's, are exploring other literacies/skills (e.g., creativity and innovation, critical thinking and problem solving, communication and collaboration, and technological) required by students in the 21st century (Partnership For 21st Century Skills, 2011). The integration of these skills is becoming an increasingly important consideration in large-scale assessment, since many assessment programs are moving toward or are implementing computer-based test administration, which has the potential to allow for measurement of skills that cannot be assessed through the paper-based assessment format.

Curriculum Linkages

Once the construct has been defined, decisions must be made about the specific content to be assessed. Due to inherent limitations of large-scale assessment, not all curriculum learning expectations lend themselves to measurement by large-scale assessment methods. For example, having students identify elements of their writing that need improvement using feedback from their teacher and peers is problematic in most large-scale assessment programs due to the constraints of time and the need for consistent administration across the jurisdiction. Consequently, decisions need to be made about the elements of the curriculum that are to be included as part of the construct to be measured. Elements that are difficult to measure in large-scale assessment are better measured at the classroom level.

It is important, therefore, both for test developers and educators whose students participate in the testing, to have information that identifies the learning expectations that will and will not be measured by the assessment. In other words, the linkages between the curriculum and the test need to be clearly demonstrated. Table 2, an extract from EQAO's Primary Division framework document, identifies clusters of Grade 3 mathematics curriculum expectations in the strand of data management and probability for which test items will be developed. In this strand, five items are developed: three multiple-choice and two open-response items. The operational mathematics test consists of 28 multiple-choice and eight open-response items. Expectations that cannot be measured by EQAO's large-scale assessment are italicized.

TABLE 2: Curriculum Linkages — Grade 3 Mathematics Expectations

Curriculum Expectation Number	Strand: Data Management and Probability	
3m75	**Data Management and Probability, Overall Expectation 1** collect and organize categorical or discrete primary data and display the data using charts and graphs, including vertical and horizontal bar graphs, with labels ordered appropriately along horizontal axes, as needed	
1	**Data Management and Probability, Specific Expectations for Overall 1: Collection and Organization of Data**	
3m78	demonstrate an ability to organize objects into categories, by sorting and classifying objects using two or more attributes simultaneously (Sample problem: Sort a collection of buttons by size, colour, and number of holes.)	
3m79	*collect data by conducting a simple survey about themselves, their environment, issues in their school or community, or content from another subject*	
3m80	collect and organize categorical or discrete primary data and display the data in charts, tables, and graphs (including vertical and horizontal bar graphs), with appropriate titles and labels and with labels ordered appropriately along horizontal axes, as needed, using many-to-one correspondence (e.g., in a pictograph, one car sticker represents 3 cars; on a bar graph, one square represents 2 students) (*Sample problem:* Graph data related to the eye colour of students in the class, using a vertical bar graph. Why does the scale on the vertical axis include values that are not in the set of data?)	
3m76	**Data Management and Probability, Overall Expectation 2** read, describe, and interpret primary data presented in charts and graphs, including vertical and horizontal bar graphs	
2	**Data Management and Probability, Specific Expectations for Overall 2: Data Relationships**	
3m81	read primary data presented in charts, tables, and graphs (including vertical and horizontal bar graphs), then describe the data using comparative language, and describe the shape of the data (e.g., "Most of the data are at the high end."; "All of the data values are different.")	3 MC 2 OR
3m82	interpret and draw conclusions from data presented in **charts, tables, and graphs**	
3m83	demonstrate an understanding of mode (e.g., "The mode is the value that shows up most often on a graph."), and identify the mode in a set of data	

MC: number of multiple-choice items
OR: number of open-response items

TABLE 2: Curriculum Linkages — Grade 3 Mathematics Expectations (continued)

Curriculum Expectation Number	Strand Data Management and Probability
3m77	**Data Management and Probability, Overall Expectation 3** predict and *investigate* the frequency of a specific outcome in a simple probability experiment
3	**Data Management and Probability, Specific Expectations for Overall 3: Probability**
3m84	predict the frequency of an outcome in a simple probability experiment or game (e.g., "I predict that an even number will come up 5 times and an odd number will come up 5 times when I roll a number cube 10 times."), then *perform the experiment,* and compare the results with the predictions, using mathematical language
3m85	demonstrate, *through investigation,* an understanding of fairness in a game and relate this to the occurrence of equally likely outcomes

Source: Adapted from EQAO's Framework: Assessment of Reading, Writing and Mathematics, Primary Division (Grades 1–3) (2007a), p.30; © by EQAO, used with permission.

Content and Timing

In addition to the curricular connections, it is important that educators and students understand the composition and timing of the test. The framework document provides information about the number of closed- and/or open-response test items (questions/challenges) each student will address (including field-test items where appropriate and whether or not they contribute to a student's score) and the number of test booklets or test sessions involved. Statements also need to be made concerning whether the test is timed (meaning there is a strict time limit) or untimed (meaning that additional time is available within given practical or reasonable constraints), the expected amount of time required to complete the test (younger students usually write in shorter time blocks than older students) and the number of sittings. Most large-scale assessment programs also provide additional time for students who require a time accommodation. In addition, information should be provided about the time of year of testing. Will the test be administered at the beginning, the end, or at some point during the school year? Table 3, an extract from EQAO's Primary Division framework document, identifies the number and type of operational items (items that count toward a student's result) and field-test items (those that do not count toward a student's result).

TABLE 3: Number and Type of Items — Primary Division (Grade 3)

READING

	Multiple-Choice Items	Open-Response Items	Total Items
Operational Items	26	10	36
Field-Test Items	10	2	12
Total Reading Items for Each Student	36	12	48

WRITING

	Multiple-Choice Items	Writing Prompts	Total Items
Operational Items	8	3	11
Field-Test Items	1	1	2
Total Writing Items for Each Student	9	4	13

MATHEMATICS

	Multiple-Choice Items	Open-Response Items	Total Items
Operational Items	28	8	36
Field-Test Items	4	1	5
Total Mathematics Items for Each Student	32	9	41

Source: Adapted from EQAO's Framework: Assessment of Reading, Writing and Mathematics, Primary Division (Grades 1–3) (2007a), pp.17-19; © by EQAO, used with permission.

Item Development

The framework document should briefly describe the approach to be used for developing test items. For instance, will the items be developed "internally" by the testing organization? Will teachers be involved in item writing? It should be emphasized that the quality of the items upon which the assessment is built is the foundation of a successful assessment program. During correspondence, Dr. Todd Rogers, Professor Emeritus, University of Alberta, stressed the importance of item development in large-scale assessment:

> Relevant items, which together represent the construct or the domain of interest defined by the content and cognitive skills to be measured, are the cornerstone of an excellent assessment program.

More information about item development is provided in Chapter 3.

Field Testing

Although the framework document will likely not go into great detail on the topic of field testing, it is important to at least make a statement as to whether or not field testing of test items is conducted. Most large-scale assessment programs include some form of field testing which may involve embedding field-test items in assessment booklets or administering separate blocks of field-test items at the same time as the assessment or at a different time. More information about field testing is provided in Chapter 4.

Accommodations, Modifications, Special Provisions, Deferrals and Exemptions

All students must have the opportunity to demonstrate the knowledge and skills they possess. Hence, every large-scale assessment program is faced with the challenge of fairly involving students who are at varying stages of acquiring the language of the test or who have special education needs. The framework document, therefore, should indicate any allowable special provisions, such as extra time for students for whom the language of the test is a second language and special settings (e.g., separate room) and accommodations such as presentation formats (e.g., Braille, large-print, coloured-paper versions of the test) and response formats (e.g., computer, scribing) for students with special needs. Accommodations are defined in EQAO's accommodations guides (2014d, e & f) as

> ...changes in the way the assessment is administered or the way in which a student with special education needs responds to its components. These do not alter the content of the assessment or affect validity or reliability. (p. 1)

In cases where the allowable accommodations do not address the student's needs, or if the required accommodations will result in a modification of the test, then exemptions from testing may be permitted (except for the Grade 9 mathematics assessment). EQAO's accommodations guides (2014d, e & f) define modifications as

> ...changes to the content of the assessment. These are not permitted, because they affect the validity and reliability of the assessment. (p. 1)

Ontario provincial assessments do not allow modifications, although some jurisdictions' assessment programs do. For instance, based on the Individuals with Disabilities Education Act (1997) and the No Child Left Behind Act (2001) all U.S. states provide alternate forms of assessment for students who cannot participate in the standard state tests, even with accommodations (U.S. Department of Education, 2004). More information on this topic is provided in Chapter 10.

Often, in the case of high-stakes certification tests, there is the option to defer a student to a subsequent sitting of the assessment. This alternative is usually taken when a student has insufficient facility in the language of the test to have any chance of success. In most large-scale assessment programs, there is also a process for exempting students who cannot meaningfully participate. All of these special circumstances should be described in the framework document. It should be noted that some jurisdictions publish separate, detailed guides related to accommodations and exemptions. EQAO's guides are posted on the agency Web site at www.eqao.com.

Alternate Assessments

As previously noted, some jurisdictions provide alternate forms of assessments to measure the learning progress of the relatively small number of students with special education needs who are unable to participate in the regular testing situation. Examples of alternate assessments include portfolios of student work, projects, oral assessments and courses. In Ontario, a successful result on the Ontario Secondary School Literacy Test (OSSLT) is one of 32 requirements for secondary school graduation. Although not designed as an alternate form of assessment for students with special education needs, there is an alternate way that students can satisfy the literacy requirement: successful completion of the Ontario Secondary School Literacy Course (OSSLC), which is available under particular circumstances. Information about the availability of alternate assessments should also be recorded in the framework document. This topic, including information about the OSSLC, is explored further in Chapter 10.

Scoring

A framework document should indicate, in general terms, how the various test item types will be scored. Closed-response items (e.g., multiple-choice, true/false) are most commonly machine scored, while students' open responses are usually scored manually in one location or through distributed scoring (although computer scoring of open responses using artificial intelligence is beginning to show promise). Open-response scoring requires that a set of scoring rules be established to ensure consistent scoring. Scoring rubrics (referred to as scoring guides in some jurisdictions) must be developed for each open-response item. It is also useful to show sample rubrics in a framework document. There are two types of scoring rubrics, generic and item-specific. Generic rubrics are general rubrics that remain constant from one assessment to the next and help to ensure comparability across years. Item-specific rubrics are developed from the generic rubrics but reflect the specific item or task. Table 4 provides examples of generic rubrics for topic development and use of conventions in writing. These rubrics are taken from the EQAO's framework document for the Primary Division (Grades 1-3). More information about scoring is presented in Chapter 6.

TABLE 4: Generic Rubrics for Writing Tasks

	TOPIC DEVELOPMENT
Code	**Descriptor**
Blank	Blank: nothing written or drawn in the space provided
Illegible/ Off Topic	Illegible: cannot be read; completely crossed out/erased; not written in English **OR** Irrelevant content: does not attempt assigned prompt (e.g., comment on the task, drawings, "?", "!", "I don't know") **OR** Off topic: no relationship of written work to assigned prompt **OR** Errors in conventions prevent communication
Code 10	Response is not developed; ideas and information are limited and unclear. Organization* is random with no links between ideas. Response has a limited relationship to the assigned task.**
Code 20	Response is minimally developed with few ideas and little information. Organization* is minimal with weak links between ideas. Response is partly related to the assigned task.**
Code 30	Response has a clear focus, adequately developed with ideas and supporting details. Organization* is simple or mechanical with adequate links between ideas. Response is clearly related to the assigned task.**
Code 40	Response has a clear focus, well-developed with sufficient specific and relevant ideas and supporting details. Organization* is logical and coherent with effective links between ideas. Response has a thorough relationship to the assigned task.**

* Organization refers to the sequencing of information and events. The links may be explicit (e.g., transition words) or implicit (the right information at the right time).
** Task refers to form, purpose and audience.

TABLE 4: Generic Rubrics for Writing Tasks (continued)

USE OF CONVENTIONS

Code	Descriptor
Blank	Blank: nothing written or drawn in the space provided
Illegible/ Off Topic	Illegible: cannot be read; completely crossed out/erased; not written in English **OR** Errors in conventions prevent[1] communication
Code 10	Errors in conventions interfere[2] with communication **OR** Insufficient evidence[3] to assess the use of conventions
Code 20	Errors in conventions do not interfere[4] with communication
Code 30	Conventions are used appropriately[5] to communicate

CONVENTIONS refers to grammar, usage, spelling and punctuation.

[1] **Prevent:** Errors prevent understanding. The reader cannot determine what the piece of writing is saying.
[2] **Interfere:** Reading rhythm is constantly stopped by errors. There is so much re-reading that the reader has difficulty recalling what the piece of writing said overall.
[3] **Insufficient evidence:** The student has not written enough to assess his/her use of conventions. A minimum of two sentences is required.
[4] **Do not interfere:** Reading rhythm may be interrupted by errors, but the information can be understood.
[5] **Conventions are used appropriately:** Use of conventions from the curriculum is evident. Some errors may exist, but the reader rarely slows down when reading.

Source: Adapted from EQAO's Framework: Assessment of Reading, Writing and Mathematics, Primary Division (Grades 1–3) (2007a), pp.32-33; © *by EQAO, used with permission.*

Reporting

The framework document should also give some indication of the type of reporting that will result from the assessment. For instance, will there be individual student reports? Will there be school and/or school board reports? Will there be provincial/state or national reports? What information will the different reports contain?

The methods of reporting should be consistent with the purpose(s) of the assessment and should reflect decisions about how scores are to be interpreted: whether the assessment is norm- or criterion-referenced (discussed earlier in this chapter).

Maintaining Consistency

It is essential to be able to demonstrate that the assessments are fair and consistent from year to year in terms of the subject content and the cognitive skills being assessed. In addition, in order that students, educators and the public have confidence in the assessment results, steps should be taken to ensure the consistency of test administration from year to year, especially if results are to be compared over time. Assessment programs deal with the issues of consistency in a variety of ways. Depending on the program, the measures taken may include the following:

- Using the same or similar assessment blueprint from year to year
- Maintaining the same test format from year to year
- Including items on an assessment that have been previously field tested to equate (compare/link) student performance from one year to the next
- Re-using test items from previous test administrations (This may involve using a set of anchor items that are used from year to year.)
- Using appropriate equating methods (See Chapter 8 for more information on equating.)
- Having consistent, published administration and accommodation procedures

- Instituting procedures to monitor assessment administration in schools
- Implementing procedures to ensure consistent, reliable and valid scoring of student work
- Implementing procedures to ensure consistent, reliable and valid data processing and statistical scoring, as well as documentation of procedures
- Monitoring databases for unusual patterns of student responses
- Conducting random checks of assessment materials on receiving them from schools
- Replicating data analyses independently

The framework document should provide general information about how consistency will be accomplished. These procedures will be elaborated more fully in subsequent chapters of this handbook.

SUMMARY

This chapter demonstrates that many decisions need to be made before designing, developing and implementing a large-scale assessment program. Documentation of these decisions and the underlying key principles in a publicly available framework document has many advantages, including helping ensure that the results are reliable and can be validly interpreted and to demonstrate that the program is both ethical and defensible.

ITEM DEVELOPMENT

CHAPTER THREE

ETHICAL CONSIDERATIONS

There are important ethical considerations in test development. The *Principles for Fair Student Assessment Practices for Education in Canada* (1993) states the following:

> Developers of assessment methods should strive to make them as fair as possible for use with students who have different backgrounds or special needs. Developers should provide the information users need to select methods appropriate to their assessment needs. (p. 13)

TEST DESIGN

Before describing the development of items, it is useful to know the nature of the test to be developed. The design of the test and the development of items and tasks that make up the test will be the product of several factors, including the purpose(s) of the test, the amount of available time for testing, the precision of the scores required and the plan for reporting. The EQAO assessments will be used to illustrate how these factors influence the test design.

As mentioned in the Introduction, EQAO conducted a major review of all aspects of its large-scale assessment program after several years of assessments. One important consideration was that the assessments required a significant amount of class instructional time and hence was a burden for schools. In the early years of the assessment program, the Primary and Junior assessments of Reading, Writing and Mathematics involved about 12 hours of testing over a two-week period; the Grade 9 Mathematics Assessment took up about five hours of classroom time over a two-week period; and the OSSLT required about five hours of class time and was administered over a two-day period. The reviewers recommended that the amount of testing time be reduced by at least one-half. In the re-designed assessments the number of test items was dramatically reduced as was the amount of testing time with no loss of precision given the assessments' purposes.

Today, the Primary and Junior assessments are designed to be administered in six hours (two hours for each of reading, writing and mathematics but not necessarily in consecutive two-hour blocks); the Grade 9 test is administered in two hours (two, 60-minute sessions) and the OSSLT is administered in two and a half hours (two, 75-minute time blocks on a single morning). Following are descriptions of the assessments. It should be noted that each assessment has multiple forms that contain the same operational items but different field-test items.

The Primary and Junior assessments (English and French) each consist of three booklets: two in language arts and one in mathematics. Each of the two language arts booklets contains both operational and field-test reading and writing tasks. The operational component contains one long narrative reading selection (450-500 words in Primary; 650-700 words in Junior) followed by ten multiple-choice and two open-response items. The reading component also contains four short reading selections in different genres: narrative, informational text, poem and graphic text (200-250 words in Primary; 300-350 words in Junior) each followed by four multiple-choice and two open-response items. The operational writing component requires one one-page and two half-page responses (Primary) and one two-page and two one-page responses (Junior), as well as eight multiple-choice items. In mathematics, the operational component contains 28 multiple-choice and eight open-response items. As in all EQAO assessments, a small number of field-test items are embedded in the Primary and Junior assessments and account for no more than 20 percent of a student's time on the test.

The Grade 9 Assessment of Mathematics (English and French) consists of two booklets. The booklets contain a total of 24 multiple-choice and seven open-response operational items. A small number of field-test items (three multiple-choice and one open-response) are embedded in the test for possible use on future assessments.

The OSSLT (English and French), which measures whether a student has acquired the cross-curricular literacy (reading and writing) skills identified in *The Ontario Curriculum* to the end of Grade 9, contains two language booklets. Like all EQAO assessments, a small number of field-test items are embedded in the test for possible use on future assessments. The operational reading component contains one long narrative reading selection (450-500 words) followed by eight multiple-choice and one open-response item. There are also four short reading selections (information paragraph, news report, dialogue (200-250 words) and graphic text (maximum 150 words) each followed by five or six multiple-choice items and three with an open-response item (the dialogue has two open-response items). The operational writing component requires two six-line, one one-page and one two-page responses, as well as eight multiple-choice items.

TEST DEVELOPMENT APPROACHES

Once the framework document has been developed, work can proceed on deciding how to acquire or develop the testing instruments. There are three approaches for developing items and constructing assessment instruments:

- Selecting assessments off-the-shelf
- Using customized assessments
- Developing homegrown assessments

Many practical issues will come into play in making this decision, including the availability of human resources, financial resources, technical expertise and the timeframe involved. Redfield (2001) explains that already-existing (off-the-shelf) commercial tests can be purchased from a vendor, thereby allowing test implementation in a relatively short timeframe. Another advantage of purchasing commercial tests is that often they are accompanied by normative data, as well as administration, scoring, interpretation and technical guides and reports. However, if the assessment program is meant to measure the learning expectations of a given jurisdiction, the linkages between the test's items and the jurisdiction's curriculum may not be a perfect or close match. As a result, this approach to securing a test may not be acceptable to stakeholders. All of the items will not be relevant to the domain of interest, and those that are will likely not fully represent the domain as specified in the test blueprint for the jurisdiction.

If purchasing a test off the shelf is not palatable, then the customized assessment approach may be selected in which a vendor is contracted to conduct aspects of the assessment program. For example, the vendor may be contracted to develop items and test forms, administer the test forms to students, score student work, analyze test results and/or produce reports. Very often when organizations or jurisdictions consider contracting, a Request for Proposals (RFP) process is established to consider whether an appropriate single contractor or multiple contractors can be identified to accomplish the work. This approach may seem straightforward and appealing, as many of the functions become the responsibility of the contractor.

As attractive as this approach may be at first glance, there is still much work to be done by the contracting organization if the assessment program is to be successful. For instance, the RFP, upon which a final contract will be built, needs to detail all of the requirements of the testing program; this requires a great deal of time and effort. To provide an example, if the contractor is to deliver item development services, then the test blueprint should be provided, including the number and types of items that are required to fill the test form(s). If the contractor is expected to develop extra items (overage) to allow for a certain proportion that may be rejected by the contracting organization, this needs to be specified in the RFP. Additional blueprint specifications (e.g., expected item difficulties) and production specifications (e.g., fonts, font sizes) may also be required.

Those considering the contracting approach must also be aware that a key and heavy responsibility is that of contract management. It must be understood that someone with management authority on the part of the contracting organization and likely a task team will need to devote a significant amount of time to managing the contract. Many publications (e.g., Porter-Roth, 2001; Aschbacher, 1989) provide useful guidelines for RFP development. Examples of large-scale assessment RFP's are also available (e.g., Utah State Office of Education, 2012; Nebraska Department of Education, 2012; New York State Education Department, 2013a; EQAO, 2013a).

The homegrown or in-house approach means that the assessments are designed, developed, administered, scored, analyzed and/or reported by the province, state, agency or organization. For example, some provinces/states have a division within the Ministry/Department of Education that is responsible for all aspects of assessment. Others contract out part of the work but complete the rest in-house. While the costs associated with the homegrown approach are high, this approach will involve teachers from the jurisdiction to develop the items to be used and to score the students responses to the open-response items. The involvement of teachers increases the transparency of the process and leads to greater acceptance by educators in the jurisdiction.

EQAO has had experience with both the homegrown and customized approaches. In its early years, the agency used the homegrown approach for test item development and test construction; psychometric aspects such as year-to-year equating were contracted out. Over a five-year period, beginning in 2003, EQAO worked with two different contractors that at different times provided item development services. However, the agency has since returned to a homegrown approach in which all aspects of the assessment are done in-house. This means that EQAO has developed internal staff expertise in the key areas of item and test development, scoring, psychometrics and reporting. The agency continues to contract out services such as printing, distribution and receipt of student booklets, scanning the responses to multiple-choice items, and replication of the statistical/psychometric work of calibration and equating. (More information about calibration and equating is provided in Chapter 8.) As indicated above, EQAO's homegrown approach means that the agency continues to involve Ontario educators in all aspects of its assessments, a point that is highlighted throughout this handbook.

The homegrown approach demands that the organization has professional expertise in a variety of specialized areas. The primary advantage of this approach is that the organization has complete, direct control over all aspects of assessment, while recognizing that detailed planning, coordination and quality control involves significant human resources and effort.

ASSESSMENT BLUEPRINT

Once the decision has been made about the approach for designing and implementing an assessment and the testing parameters have been set out, one of the first tasks is to establish the assessment blueprint or test specifications. The assessment blueprint is important for five reasons:

- First, the assessment blueprint indicates the number and/or proportion and type of test items (i.e., closed- and open-response) that will be developed to measure the assessment's content knowledge and skills.

- Second, it provides a guide for item writers who need to know the learning expectations or skills for which they are developing items, as well as their levels of difficulty.

- Third, it is important that there is consistency of forms so that the test will be consistent from one year to the next in terms of the content measured and the relative difficulty of the test items.

- Fourth, for any given assessment in any given year there may be more than a single test form developed. By following a blueprint, there is greater likelihood that the test forms will reflect the same learning expectations. (In Ontario, for example, parallel tests are developed for administration in January for first-semester Grade 9 mathematics students and in May/June for students in the second semester or in full-year courses.)

- Fifth, while all "strands" of the curriculum are assessed each year, it is likely not possible to measure all the curriculum learning expectations within each strand in any one large-scale assessment. Further, as mentioned in the previous chapter, the curriculum expectations that cannot be measured using the present assessment mode need to be identified prior to developing the assessment blueprint (see Table 2). Consequently, a sample of measurable learning expectations within each strand is selected for item development for one year and another possibly overlapping sample of measureable learning expectations within the same strand is selected for the next year. By documenting and tracking the learning expectations that have been measured over the years and using that information when targeting expectations for development in subsequent years, one can ensure good coverage of the measurable learning expectations over time. An added advantage of sampling from the curriculum in this way is that teachers will not be able to teach only to selected learning expectations; they will need to cover all curriculum areas to ensure students are adequately prepared for the test. This discourages a narrowing of the curriculum.

It is useful to have the assessment blueprint reviewed by experienced educators and test developers prior to item development to ensure it matches the expectations of the curriculum and demonstrates adequate coverage of it. Having psychometricians review the blueprint is also important to ensure there will be a sufficient number of items for equating and to be able to report reliable results that can be validly interpreted.

There are different levels of assessment blueprints that differ in terms of the amount of detail included in them. Some large-scale assessment programs rely exclusively on a general blueprint to guide item development.

TABLE 5: Sample General Blueprint — Grade 9 Assessment of Mathematics

APPROXIMATE NUMBER OF ITEMS BY TYPE			
	Multiple-Choice Items	Open-Response Items	Total Items
Operational Items	24	7	31
Field-Test Items	3	1	4
Total Items for Each Student	27	8	35

APPROXIMATE NUMBER OF RAW SCORE POINTS AND PERCENTAGE OF TOTAL RAW SCORE POINTS BY ITEM TYPE		
Operational Item Type	Number of Raw Score Points	Percentage of Total Raw Score Points
Multiple-Choice	24	46%
Open-Response	28	54%
Total	52	100%

Source: Adapted from EQAO's Framework: Grade 9 Assessment of Mathematics (2009), p.13; © by EQAO, used with permission.

Best practice suggests that a general blueprint should be provided as an overview for public consumption. However, test item developers need to have more specific information about the learning expectations that will be targeted for the specific assessment. Consequently, a second more detailed blueprint is needed. Table 5 and Table 6 are examples of general and specific blueprints, respectively.

The general blueprint provides information about the overall number of multiple-choice and open-response items, as well as the number and percentage of score points by item type.

The sample specific blueprint indicates the number of multiple-choice and open-response items associated with the two clusters of learning expectations in the Number Sense and Algebra strand for Grade 9 mathematics. The first cluster includes four specific learning expectations related to demonstrating an understanding of the exponent rules of multiplication and division and applying the rules to simplify expressions. The second cluster includes nine specific learning expectations related to manipulating numerical and polynomial expressions, and solving first degree equations. As before, parts of the specific learning expectations that cannot be measured in the assessment are presented in italics. Two multiple-choice items are used to measure the learner expectations in the first cluster. One of these items measures knowledge and understanding (KU), and the other item measures application (AP). Three multiple-choice items and one open-response item are used to measure the learner expectations in the second cluster. One multiple-choice item measures knowledge and understanding, one measures application, and the third measures thinking/problem solving (TH); the open-response item is mapped to the cognitive skill of application. These items will measure one of the specific learning expectations in the cluster. As mentioned before, while there will always be items for the cluster, the specific learning expectations measured within a cluster will differ from one year to the next.

TABLE 6: Specific Blueprint — Grade 9 Academic Mathematics

Ministry Code	Expectations	MC Total = 24	OR Total = 7	Skills KU	AP	TH
	Number Sense and Algebra Strand					
NAV.01	**Number Sense and Algebra Overall Expectation 1** demonstrate an understanding of the exponent rules of multiplication and division, and apply them to simplify expressions					
1	**Number Sense and Algebra Specific Expectations for Overall 1: Operating with Exponents**					
NA1.01	substitute into and evaluate algebraic expressions involving exponents (i.e., evaluate expressions involving natural-number exponents with rational-number bases [e.g., evaluate $(3/2)^3$ by hand and 9.8^3 by using a calculator]) (*Sample problem:* A movie theatre wants to compare the volumes of popcorn in two containers, a cube with edge length 8.1 cm and a cylinder with radius 4.5 cm and height 8.0 cm. Which container holds more popcorn?)	2 MC		1 MC 1/2	1 MC 2/3	
NA1.02	describe the relationship between the algebraic and geometric representations of a single-variable term up to degree three [i.e., length, which is one dimensional, can be represented by x; area, which is two dimensional, can be represented by $(x)(x)$ or x^2; volume, which is three dimensional, can be represented by $(x)(x)(x)$, $(x^2)(x)$, or x^3]					
NA1.03	*derive, through the investigation and examination of patterns, the exponent rules for multiplying and dividing monomials,* and apply these rules in expressions involving one and two variables with positive exponents					
NA1.04	*extend the multiplication rule to derive* and understand the power of a power rule, and apply it to simplify expressions involving one and two variables with positive exponents					
NAV.02	**Number Sense and Algebra Overall Expectation 2** manipulate numerical and polynomial expressions, and solve first-degree equations					
2	**Number Sense and Algebra Specific Expectations for Overall 2: Manipulating Expressions and Solving Equations**					
NA2.01	simplify numerical expressions involving integers and rational numbers, with and without the use of technology					

TABLE 6: Specific Blueprint — Grade 9 Academic Mathematics (continued)

Ministry Code	Expectations	MC Total = 24	OR Total = 7	Skills KU	Skills AP	Skills TH
	Number Sense and Algebra Specific Expectations for Overall 2 (continued)					
NA2.02	solve problems requiring the manipulation of expressions arising from applications of percent, ratio, rate, and proportion					
NA2.03	relate their understanding of inverse operations to squaring and taking the square root, and apply inverse operations to simplify expressions and solve equations					
NA2.04	add and subtract polynomials with up to two variables [e.g., $(2x - 5) + (3x + 1)$, $(3x^2y + 2xy^2) + (4x^2y - 6xy^2)$], using a variety of tools (e.g., algebra tiles, computer algebra systems, paper and pencil)					
NA2.05	multiply a polynomial by a monomial involving the same variable [e.g., $2x(x + 4)$, $2x^2(3x^2 - 2x + 1)$], using a variety of tools (e.g., algebra tiles, diagrams, computer algebra systems, paper and pencil)					
NA2.06	expand and simplify polynomial expressions involving one variable [e.g., $2x(4x + 1) - 3x(x + 2)$], using a variety of tools (e.g., algebra tiles, computer algebra systems, paper and pencil)	3 MC	1 OR (AP)	1 MC 1/2	1 MC 2/3	1 MC 3/4
NA2.07	solve first-degree equations, including equations with fractional coefficients, using a variety of tools (e.g., computer algebra systems, paper and pencil) and strategies (e.g., the balance analogy, algebraic strategies)					
NA2.08	rearrange formulas involving variables in the first degree, with and without substitution (e.g., in analytic geometry, in measurement) (*Sample problem:* A circular garden has a circumference of 30 m. What is the length of a straight path that goes through the centre of this garden?)					
NA2.09	solve problems that can be modelled with first-degree equations, and compare algebraic methods to other solution methods (*Sample problem:* Solve the following problem in more than one way: Jonah is involved in a walkathon. His goal is to walk 25 km. He begins at 9:00 a.m. and walks at a steady rate of 4 km/h. How many kilometres does he still have left to walk at 1:15 p.m. if he is to achieve his goal?)					
	Total Number of Mathematics Items on Test to be Developed by Item Type and Skill	24 MC	7 OR	8 MC 0 OR	9 MC 4 OR	7 MC 3 OR

MC: Multiple-choice item
OR: Open-response item
KU: Knowledge and understanding
AP: Application
TH: Thinking
1/2: Distinguishes between a Level 1 and Level 2 (easy)
2/3: Distinguishes between a Level 2 and Level 3 (medium)
3/4: Distinguishes between a Level 3 and Level 4 (difficult)

Source: Adapted from EQAO's records; © by EQAO, used with permission.

ITEM DEVELOPMENT

Item Formats

Item formats can be classified as selected-response, open-response (constructed-response) and performance items.

- Selected-response items require students to select the correct or best answer from a list of alternatives. Multiple-choice, matching and true-false formats are common examples of selected-response items.
- Constructed-response items require students to generate their own responses. These items include short and long written responses of various types.
- Performance items require students to apply their knowledge, skills and abilities in the context of, for example, laboratory experiments, mathematics investigations, portfolios and performances of various kinds.

There are many misconceptions about item types and their uses. For example, some educators believe that selected-response items can only be used to gather information about basic knowledge and that deriving information about higher mental processes such as application of knowledge, interpretation, analysis, synthesis, critical thinking and thinking/problem solving can only be accessed using constructed-response and performance items. This, of course, is an over-simplification. Although selected-response items do lend themselves well to gathering information about the students' acquisition of knowledge, if skillfully developed, this item type can also be used to assess higher mental processes (see Rodríguez, 2002 and Haladyna, 1999, for example). Furthermore, if attention is given to students' common errors and misconceptions when developing distractors (incorrect answer choices) for multiple-choice items, then valuable information can be obtained about student learning needs by conducting an error analysis.

Number of Items

Decisions about the number and types of items will hinge on the purpose(s) of the test, the use of the information derived from it, the amount of available classroom time for testing given the age of the students and the cost and time required for scoring open-response items. It is also important to note that several items or tasks are required to be able to report confidently about student achievement for any category of interest (e.g., skill areas in language or strands in mathematics). Dr. Mark Reckase, Professor Emeritus, Michigan State University provides a good example of this concept.

> Imagine a sandbox with an unknown object buried beneath the sand. If you push a single rod (probe) into the sand you may or may not touch the object. Even if you do, it is highly unlikely you could identify it from one probe. Only after using several probes can one discover the object's shape. The same thing applies in testing. A single item or measure (probe) will usually not reveal much about a student's knowledge or ability. Only after using several items can one estimate a student's achievement.

A good rule of thumb is that at least ten well-constructed items are needed to report confidently and validly on any category of achievement, and only if the items represent an appropriate cross-section of the relevant learning expectations (including an appropriate range of item difficulty) in the achievement category.

Universal Design

A key to ensuring that assessment materials are made as fair as possible for use with students who have different backgrounds or special needs is the concept of universal design. Thompson, Johnstone and Thurlow (2002) explain that the ultimate objective of universal design is to be as inclusive as possible. The authors state that:

> Universally designed assessments are designed and developed from the beginning to allow participation of the widest possible range of students, and to result in valid inferences about performance for all students who participate in the assessment. Universally designed assessments add a dimension of fairness to the testing process. (p. 7)

They go on to explain that underlying this principle is the premise that each child in school is a part of the population to be tested, and that testing results should not be affected by disability, gender, race or language of the test:

> This does not mean that standards should be relaxed or that constructs to be measured should be changed (such changes would constitute test modifications). Items on a universally-designed standards-based assessment must be aligned to the content and achievement standards with the same depth and breadth of coverage, and the same cognitive complexity as the standards specify. The emphasis can be on accessibility using different formats, technologies, and designs to include all students. (p. 9)

Thompson et al. (2002) identify the following elements of universal design that should be addressed during item development:

- Test items should be accessible and non-biased.
- Test items should be amenable to accommodations.
- Instructions and procedures should be simple and clear.
- Readability and comprehensibility should be maximized.

Popham (2001) listed four elements and questions (adapted here) that should be considered and asked during item development to aid in avoiding bias.

- **Curricular congruence:** Would students' responses to this and other items allow one to determine whether or not they have mastered the learning expectations being measured?
- **Instructional sensitivity:** Is it likely that most of the students will be able to respond correctly to the item?
- **Out-of-school factors:** Is the item free of content that would advantage or disadvantage students (e.g., socioeconomic status)?
- **Personal factors:** Is the item free of content that might offend or disadvantage students because of their personal characteristics (e.g., race, gender, disability)? (p. 93)

When planning item development, it is important to consider the accommodations that will be used to facilitate student access to the test by allowing special presentation and response formats beyond the paper-and-pencil format used by most students. (Online assessments are not dealt with here.) Usually, the students requiring special formats are students with special education needs and students who are in the early stages of learning the language of instruction. The use of accommodations (e.g., Braille) will be facilitated if certain features are avoided during item development (Thompson et al., 2002):

- Irrelevant graphics or pictures that may be distracting or misleading
- Vertical or diagonal text that do not lend themselves to Braille
- Keys and legends located to the left or bottom of the item, where they are more difficult to locate in Braille formats
- Graphic representations (such as maps) that do not also have verbal or textual descriptions that can be translated into Braille
- Distracting or purely decorative pictures, which take attention away from the content of the item (p. 13)

Assessment instructions and procedures should be simple, clear and easy to understand. All students should have the opportunity to demonstrate what they know and can do. Readability of the assessment materials, therefore, is a critical element of test item development. Rakow and Gee (1987) define readability as "an estimate of probability of comprehension by a particular group" (p. 28). Often, readability is calculated by taking into consideration the length of the sentence and the number of difficult/multi-syllabic words. In theory, shorter sentences and easier words translate into more readable texts. The following guidelines should be considered to enhance readability (adapted from Gaster & Clark, 1995):

- Use simple, commonly used words.
- Avoid unnecessary verbiage.
- Avoid technical terms, but provide clear definitions when they must be used (unless terminology is expected in the curriculum).

- Avoid using compound sentences wherever possible; break them down into shorter sentences.

Consideration of these guidelines should be given in the context of the subject area involved. For instance, in mathematics there are terms that students should know; however, to ensure that level of language is not being tested rather than mathematics knowledge and skills, a good rule of thumb is that non-mathematical wording should be at a lower level than the grade being tested. This rule of thumb applies to all subject areas. In addition to the works referenced in this chapter, there are several other good resources that provide guidance on item development in various formats (see Haladyna & Rodriguez, 2013, for example).

Consideration of the various aspects of universal design during item and test development, bias reviews involving educators who work with students with special needs and other stakeholders representing the various demographic and social realities of the jurisdiction, and field testing of items with a broad cross section of the target student population will contribute significantly to the development of an assessment that is fair and accessible to the widest possible range of students. Test accommodations are discussed at greater length in Chapter 5 of this handbook.

Reading Selections

Acquiring reading selections for large-scale reading assessments is accomplished in a variety of ways. Some jurisdictions and testing companies believe an effective approach is to commission the writing of reading selections. They believe that by doing so the selections will conform to detailed specifications, and there will be no subsequent issues related to obtaining copyright. Other jurisdictions and organizations believe that finding already-published reading selections and either using them as is or adapting them is the better approach. They believe that since the pieces have been previously published, they are more "authentic," and they require less editing. Regardless of the approach taken, procedures will need to be established to obtain copyright permissions to use source materials and, especially, previously published selections. In addition, the implementation of a fact-checking process is a necessity to ensure all information in the reading selection is accurate.

EQAO uses a combination of these two approaches. The agency endeavors to acquire reading selections on a year-round, ongoing basis to ensure that adequate numbers of reading passages are available for its Primary (Grade 3) and Junior (Grade 6) reading assessments and the OSSLT. Approximately three-quarters of the reading passages are either selected from published sources and used as is or adapted, and about one-quarter are written by EQAO education officers or by contracted individuals (mostly experienced educators). The contracted writers receive one-half day of EQAO training that includes the specifications for the reading selections (e.g., reading types, readability and word length), information about copyright and sourcing issues and timelines for completing the work. EQAO's education officers review the passages developed by the contracted writers and provide feedback. Following revision as needed, these passages are added to the pool of reading selections.

EQAO uses the following software packages to gauge the readability of English-language reading selections in the pool: Flesch Reading Ease, Flesch Grade Level, FOG, Powers, SMOG, FORCAST and FRY. For the French language, the agency uses SATO-calibrage, software developed by the Ministry of Education in the Province of Quebec, researchers at the University of Quebec in Montreal and provincial educators in Quebec. Passages with unacceptable reading levels for the assessment are removed. The remaining selections are then reviewed following the process outlined later in this chapter under the heading Review Committees.

Role of Teachers in Item Development

Although some large-scale assessment programs rely on professional item writers to create test items, most large-scale programs involve teachers in some capacity, as they bring current pedagogy and their experience with students to the development process. In addition, the involvement of teachers sends an important message to the field: the assessment is not developed solely by bureaucrats and/or assessment specialists removed from the realities of the classroom. Involving classroom teachers in item writing brings credibility and authenticity to the testing program and also provides valuable professional development for the teachers.

Typically, teachers are not expert item writers; however, they do bring a wealth of classroom-based experience and creative ideas. With appropriate training, teachers can develop good draft items that can then be "professionalized" by experts in item development.

Teachers are involved in item development in a variety of ways. In some U.S. jurisdictions (e.g., Florida) the Department of Education employs test development contractors who hire professional/experienced item writers to draft all test items. Following submission of items to the contractor, they are reviewed and revised internally by contractor staff, and then by Department of Education staff who work with committees of state classroom teachers (Florida Department of Education, 2013). In other U.S. jurisdictions (e.g., Michigan), the state works with educator item writers to develop test items (Michigan Department of Education, 2012). The use of test development contractors is relatively rare in Canada. In most provinces, the test items are initially written by practicing teachers under the supervision of ministry of education assessment specialists (Klinger et al., 2008).

Developing Items

Many jurisdictions in the U.S. and Canada hold item-writing events, in which item developers are brought together to a central location to receive training and to draft items. With the advent of computer technology and the Internet, some jurisdictions have implemented procedures in which item writers can work from home and submit items electronically. Several vendors in the U.S. (e.g., Educational Testing Service [ETS], Kryterion, Measured Progress, Measurement Incorporated, Pearson, Prometric, The Donath Group) offer Web-based remote item authoring methodologies to facilitate item development. Regardless of the approach taken, it is necessary that the item writers be well trained to develop relevant items that together represent the domain to be assessed.

Although EQAO is currently implementing remote item authoring for one of its assessment programs as part of its move toward computer-based assessment, the main approach has been to bring item writers to a central location. The agency annually recruits and trains educators to write test items, including mathematics items, short reading and writing tasks and long writing prompts. There are separate item writing committees in both English and French for each subject and grade assessed. Each committee consists of 10 to 20 members who generally serve terms of up to five years. Approximately 20 percent of the members are rotated off the committee each year, thereby retaining a cadre of experienced writers while injecting new "blood" into the development process. A positive result of this rotation is that a number of teachers receive training and experience in item writing which they can apply in the development of classroom assessment items.

The criteria used to select item writers (adapted from *EQAO's Technical Report for the 2011-2012 Assessments,* 2013b) are as follows:

- Expert knowledge and recent classroom experience in the subject/grade curriculum
- Excellent written communication skills
- Comfort using computer word-processing software for language and mathematics given the use of laptop computers during item writing sessions
- Experience in writing instructional or classroom materials for students
- Proven ability to work collaboratively and to accept instruction and critical feedback
- Access to grade and subject classrooms to conduct item tryouts and cognitive labs

Item developers/writers and educators who will review the items are required to sign confidentiality agreements to ensure the items, including reading passages, are kept secure and confidential.

First Item-Writing Session

The item writing committees meet centrally twice per year (for two or three days in each of the fall and the winter) to write and review items. At the beginning of the first item writing session, a half-day is devoted to training which includes providing an overview of the assessment framework as a context for the item writing work, the criteria for developing relevant and effective items and information on the skills being assessed. The writing of both multiple-choice and open-response items takes a great deal of skill and experience; hence, effective training for item writers is extremely important. As part of this training, item writers are provided with detailed development guidelines that must be followed. Below are some selected EQAO general guidelines for writing effective open-response and multiple-choice items.

Open-response items and their instructions should

- be written in simple, clear language;
- elicit a range of student performance on the scoring rubric used;
- measure learning expectations that can't be easily measured by multiple-choice items;
- be developed prior to developing multiple-choice items for a reading selection (if multiple-choice items are written first, it may be difficult to create meaningful open-response items) and
- be able to be completed in four to six minutes on average (for short responses) and up to 20 minutes (for longer responses measuring writing skills).

The writers of open-response items are asked to draft item-specific rubrics using the information gained from item try-outs and cognitive labs (described next in this chapter under the sub-heading "Item Try-outs and Cognitive Labs") during the second item-writing session and during range finding (described in Chapter 6).

Multiple-choice items should

- contain one correct or best response;
- provide plausible distractors (throw-away responses are to be avoided);
- link to curriculum learning expectations as identified in the specific blueprint for the assessment;
- be written in simple, clear language;
- avoid negatives;
- present a complete task or question in the stem that could be answered without seeing the alternatives/options (in EQAO Primary assessments, sentence completions are permitted);
- have alternatives/options that are presented in a logical sequence (e.g., shortest to longest) to enhance readability;
- have alternatives/options that are parallel in language used and amount of specificity;
- be independent (the answer to one question should not provide clues to responding to another question) and
- be able to be completed in one to two minutes on average.

The balance of the first item writing session involves item writing during which time agency education officers monitor items as they are developed, respond to questions and provide feedback/critique on the draft items. Each item writer is provided with a writing assignment that identifies the learning expectations for which they are to develop items, the item types that the writer must develop, the expected difficulty of the multiple-choice items, and the distribution of students across the codes of the scoring rubrics the item writers develop for the open-response items. To ensure consistency of the items developed and appropriate curriculum and item difficulty coverage, the item writers are provided with electronic templates (item cards) that indicate the curriculum strands/skills/domains, overall and specific learning expectations and levels of difficulty expected for each of the items to be developed. The items writers enter their multiple-choice items and a rationale for the distractors and the open-response items with their scoring rubrics directly on the electronic item card. At the end of the first item-writing session, the education officers, in collaboration with EQAO editors, make revisions to the draft test items.

In Ontario, the Primary, Junior and Grade 9 assessments are reported on a four-level proficiency scale in which Level 1 is the lowest level of student achievement and Level 4 is the highest level of student achievement. These levels are aligned with the Ministry of Education's four-level curriculum achievement charts. (There is also a category, NE1, which indicates there is not enough evidence to assign a Level 1 [Primary and Junior] or insufficient achievement of curricular expectations to assign a Level 1, called Below Level 1 [Grade 9].) Level 3, which is a relatively high performance level, is the provincial standard. Student achievement on the OSSLT is either successful or unsuccessful (pass/fail).

For the Primary, Junior and Grade 9 assessments, approximately one-half of the items are written to differentiate students at the Level 2/3 threshold, as this is the cut-point for the provincial standard. About one-quarter of the test items are written at each of the Level 1/2 and Level 3/4 cut-points. For the OSSLT, the majority of the items are written to differentiate students at the successful/unsuccessful threshold.

Tables 7 and 8 are sample completed templates (item cards) for open-response and multiple-choice mathematics items, respectively. As shown, course, overall and specific expectations, category of cognitive processing, and, in the case of multiple-choice items, the expected difficulty are pre-printed on the card. The item writer enters the item/question/prompt, diagrams when needed, and, in the case of multiple-choice items, a correct answer and a rationale for each of the three distractors. As seen in Table 7, the course is Grade 9 Academic Mathematics, the item is to be referenced to the strand Measurement and Geometry and calls for thinking or problem solving. The item entered by the item writer is an open-response item presenting a cone with the top removed and with several measurements shown. The students are to determine the volume of the figure. This item is to be scored using a 4-point scoring rubric (to be discussed in Chapter 6).

TABLE 7: Sample Completed Template (Item Card) for Grade 9 Mathematics Open-Response Item

Year	Course ID:	Grade 9 Academic Mathematics	Category:	TH	Item ID
	Strand:	M	Dificulty Level:		

Overall Expectation: MV2 Students will solve problems involving the measurements of two-dimensional shapes and surface areas and volumes of three-dimensional figures.

Specific Expectation: 9D.M11 Students will solve problems involving the surface areas and volumes of prisms, pyramids, cylinders, cones, and spheres, including composite figures.

1. Cutting Cones

The figure pictured below is a cone with its top portion removed.

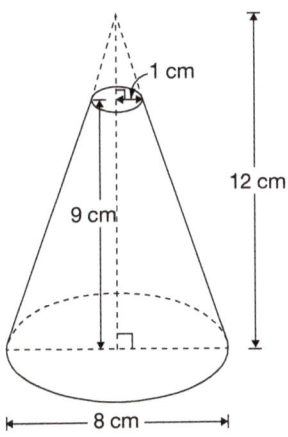

Determine the volume of this figure.

Show your work.

Strand
N – Number Sense and Algebra
R – Linear Relations
G – Analytic Geometry (Academic Only)
M – Measurement and Geometry

Category
KU – Knowledge and Understanding
AP – Application
TH – Thinking

Difficulty level
A difficulty level is not used for open-response questions, as they require answers at all four codes (10, 20, 30, 40)

Overall expectation code
Strand is included first (N, R, G, M)

Specific Expectation Code
9P Applied, Grade 9
9D – Academic, Grade 9

Source: Adapted from EQAO records; © by EQAO, used with permission.

TABLE 8: Sample Completed Template (Item Card) for Grade 9 Mathematics Multiple-choice Item

Year	Course ID:	Grade 9 Applied Mathematics	Category:	AP	Item ID
	Strand:	R	Dificulty Level:	2/3	

Overall Expectation: RV3
Students will demonstrate an understanding of constant rate of change and its connection to linear relations.

Specific Expectation: 9P.R12
Students will describe the meaning of the rate of change and the initial value for a linear relation arising from a realistic situation (e.g., the cost to rent the community gym is $40 per evening, plus $2 per person for equipment rental; the vertical intercept, 40, represents the $40 cost of renting the gym; the value of the rate of change, 2, represents the $2 cost per person), and describe a situation that could be modeled by a given linear equation (e.g., the linear equation M = 50 +6d could model the mass of a shipping package, including 50 g for the packaging material, plus 6 g per flyer added to the package)

Rationale A: Assumes 5 + 9 is rate.
Rationale B: Assumes 5 + 9 is flat fee.
Rationale C: Reverses meaning of flat fee and rate per hour.
Rationale D: Correct Answer.

---

15 For babysitting, Becky charges according to the equation $C = 5n + 9$, where C is the amount charged, in dollars, and n is the number of hours she babysits.

Which statement about this situation is correct?

A Becky charges $14 per hour.

B Becky charges a flat fee of $14.

C Becky charges an initial fee of $5, plus $9 per hour.

D Becky charges an initial fee of $9, plus $5 per hour.

Strand
N – Number Sense and Algebra
R – Linear Relations
G – Analytic Geometry (Academic Only)
M – Measurement and Geometry

Category
KU – Knowledge and Understanding
AP – Application
TH – Thinking

Difficulty level (Multiple-Choice Questions Only)
1/2 – Distinguishes between a Level 1/2 (easy)
2/3 – Distinguishes between a Level 2/3 (medium)
3/4 – Distinguishes between a Level 3/4 (difficult)

Overall expectation code
Strand is included first (N, R, G, M)

Specific Expectation Code
9P – Applied, Grade 9
9D – Academic, Grade 9

Rationale
Reasons for each answer choice (multiple-choice questions only)

Source: Adapted from EQAO records; © by EQAO, used with permission.

The second item (Table 8) is to be referenced to the Linear Relations strand, requires application, is to have a difficulty level at the 2/3 threshold and is to be referenced to the overall and specific expectations shown. The item writer enters the item together with the four options and a rationale for the distractors. Once an item writer has completed his/her item writing assignment, the items are reviewed and revised as need by the education officers in collaboration with EQAO editors. The items are then ready for item try-outs and cognitive labs.

Item Try-outs and Cognitive Labs

It is always wise to try out the items and conduct cognitive labs to obtain preliminary information about how the students approach solving the open-response tasks and the reasoning they use to select their answers to multiple-choice items. According to Zucker, Sassman and Case (2004):

> A cognitive lab is a method of studying the mental processes one uses when completing a task such as solving a mathematics problem or interpreting a passage of text. Developed and formalized using modern scientific research, cognitive labs have not only provided an effective insight into the functioning of the human mind, they also have been practically applied in the development of surveys, questionnaires, and assessments. (p. 2)

Zucker et al. explain that educators have routinely used verbal reporting or think-aloud sessions to learn where students have mastered concepts and where further assistance is needed.

Cognitive labs, in the assessment context, may be either concurrent (students verbalize their thoughts and ideas as they respond to test items) or retrospective (students provide verbal reports of their thinking processes immediately after responding to a test item). Many researchers use both the concurrent and retrospective approaches. In the early stages of item development, cognitive labs are a valuable source of information, as they suggest where items may be unclear and where revision is necessary.

EQAO primarily subscribes to the retrospective form of cognitive lab in which the item writers are provided with a standard protocol to guide interviews and record the students' information. Following the first item writing session in the fall, the item writers, who are practicing classroom teachers, conduct item try-outs and cognitive labs with the students in their own classrooms. Item writers, who are not practicing teachers, must arrange to have access to students with which to try out items and conduct cognitive labs. Tables 9.1, 9.2 and 9.3 provide sample cognitive lab protocols.

TABLE 9.1: Feedback Form: Cognitive Lab Mathematics — Multiple-Choice Items

Description of student sample:

Multiple-Choice Number	Option A Number of students	Option B Number of students	Option C Number of students	Option D Number of students	Comments and Notes (other possible distractors)

Source: Adapted from EQAO's Feedback Form: Cognitive Lab Mathematics Multiple-Choice Items; © by EQAO, used with permission.

TABLE 9.2: Feedback Form: Cognitive Lab Mathematics — Open-Response Items

Description of student sample:		
Open-Response Item Number: 00000		
Performance	Number of students	Description of Student Performance
Off Topic/Blank		
Code 10		
Code 20		
Code 30		
Code 40		
Comments and Notes:		

Source: Adapted from EQAO's Feedback Form: Cognitive Lab Mathematics Open-Response Items; © by EQAO, used with permission.

Table 9.1 illustrates a multiple-choice item cognitive lab feedback form. For each multiple-choice item, the teacher gathers information about the number of students who selects each response option, and a space is provided for comments, notes and ideas for other potential distractors. Table 9.2 demonstrates an open-response item cognitive lab feedback form. For each item, data are recorded on the number of students who performed at each score code and descriptions of student performance on the item/task. The feedback forms include spaces in which the explanations students give for choosing the given multiple-choice response or other alternative responses can be recorded.

TABLE 9.3: Item Development Cognitive Lab — Sample Focus Group Discussion Questions

OVERALL
1. What did you find easy/challenging?
2. Did you understand the question?
3. Did the question need more explanation or less wording? Any suggestions?
4. Were any phrases confusing? What were they?
5. Were there words that you did not understand? What were they?
6. If there was a picture/graphic, how did it help you? Was it clear?
7. Was there anything in the question that made you uncomfortable?
8. Overall, how could this question be improved?
9. Did you have enough time to complete the question?

MULTIPLE-CHOICE
1. Explain why you chose your answer.
2. If your first answer was not in the list of choices, explain how you arrived at it.
3. Does the correct answer stand out?
4. Did any of the choices seem irrelevant, obviously incorrect or too close to the correct answer?

OPEN-RESPONSE
1. Was the question clear?
2. Did you know what you had to do in order to answer the question?
3. How can the wording of the question be changed to make it clearer?

REFLECTION QUESTIONS FOR REVIEWING STUDENT RESPONSES

Look for patterns and trends.

1. How can the student responses inform revisions to the question?
2. Was there a range of student responses?
3. Do the student responses reflect what you anticipated?
4. Do the student responses reflect information not anticipated?
5. Based on the student responses, what is the level of difficulty of the item? (MC)
6. Does the item use age/grade appropriate language?
7. Does the item match the intended expectation?

Source: Adapted from EQAO's Item Development Cognitive Lab Sample Focus Group Discussion Questions; © by EQAO, used with permission.

Sample student responses by achievement level for open-response items may also be noted. Table 9.3 contains a list of questions to be asked of students who are interviewed about their experience in responding to the draft assessment items. Four groups of questions are used to help focus the cognitive lab on item quality and where improvements can be made.

Second Item-Writing Session

At the second item writing session in the winter, item writers consider the information from the try-outs and cognitive labs to review and revise the multiple-choice and open-response items and writing prompts they initially developed and to generate draft item-specific rubrics for open-response items. The education officers, in collaboration with the EQAO editors, then review and revise the items from the second item writing session, as needed. At this point, the items are considered to be fully developed subject to a review by an Assessment Development Committee and a Sensitivity Committee.

Review Committees

Most large-scale testing organizations incorporate committee reviews as part of the item development process. These reviews involve reviewing reading selections and items to be sure they are readable and complete in all regards and to be sure they do not favour one group of students over another. While one committee often does both reviews, some organizations use two committees, one for the review of content and the other for the review for bias/sensitivity.

EQAO has established two committees, so that one committee can focus its attention solely on content/age and curriculum appropriateness of the reading selections and items, and the second committee can focus its attention solely on the fairness of the test material for students from different cultures, genders or with special education needs. The Assessment Development Committees ensure that the items and tasks are relevant to and representative of the measureable curriculum expectations for language arts and mathematics as set out in *The Ontario Curriculum*.

TABLE 10: Assessment Development Committee Considerations for Reading Selections

GUIDING PRINCIPLE: EQAO assessments are curriculum-based. Nothing on an assessment should require knowledge or skills beyond what can reasonably be related to curriculum expectations up to and including the grade of the assessment. (OSSLT – up to and including Grade 9)

1. AGE AND GRADE APPROPRIATE
- uses appropriate age and grade vocabulary, sentence structure
- vocabulary is appropriate to the subject area/topic
- reflects an appropriate cognitive level
- is of interest to students in the grade level
- has relevance over time

2. KNOWLEDGE REQUIREMENTS
- contains accurate information
- does not rely on students possessing subject-specific content knowledge beyond the grade level
- does not rely on students possessing knowledge beyond a reasonable level of personal experience

3. PICTORIAL/GRAPHIC CONTENT
- is relevant to selection
- graphics have purpose beyond being decorative
- assists rather than misleads students who may be unfamiliar with topic
- includes both genders
- appeals to age group

4. READING SELECTION CONTENT
- is appropriate for the development of items that assess explicit, implicit and connections expectations
- is rich enough for the development of appropriate open-response items and multiple-choice items (i.e., appropriate distractors are available within the reading selection)

5. ACCESS
- is free from any content that would offend or unfairly penalize students on the basis of gender, ethnicity, religion or socio-economic status
- is not commonly used in schools
- is not readily available/accessible in current textbooks and/or school materials

6. STANDARD CANADIAN ENGLISH
- uses standard Canadian spelling
- uses plain language
- limits unfamiliar words, idiomatic expressions and/or provides a relevant context for any that are used
- explains technical terms/language in context
- avoids language, phrases or cultural innuendos that may be objectionable to a particular group of students
- limits the use of complex sentences for primary

Source: Adapted from EQAO Assessment Development Committee: Review Considerations for Reading Selections; © by EQAO, used with permission.

The Sensitivity Committees ensure that the language arts and mathematics items and tasks are free of bias and are fair and accessible to the broadest range of Ontario students.

Assessment Development Committees

There are separate Assessment Development Committees for each subject, grade level and language of testing. Each committee consists of eight to twelve Ontario educators who generally serve on the committee for up to five years. The criteria for selection of committee members are virtually the same as for item writers; however, some members (e.g., school board consultants) may not have classroom responsibilities.

The committees meet, under the supervision and guidance of EQAO staff, to provide feedback on the reading selections and the multiple-choice and open-response items referenced to selections, the writing multiple-choice items and open-response prompts, and mathematics multiple-choice and open-response tasks with regard to their age, grade and curriculum appropriateness and the extent to which they are serving the stated purpose(s) of the assessment. The committee members also provide a technical quality review by considering whether multiple-choice items have only one correct answer (keyed response), whether open-response items will elicit a range of student responses and the clarity of language. Table 10 indicates the six elements that are considered by the reading Assessment Development Committees for the reading passages selected for the reading assessments. Table 11 indicates the six elements that are considered by the Assessment Development Committees in their review of test items.

Sensitivity Committees

There are two Sensitivity Committees, one for the English-language assessments and one for the French-language assessments. Each committee consists of eight to twelve Ontario educators who generally serve on the committee for up to five years.

TABLE 11: Assessment Development Committee Considerations for Items

> **GUIDING PRINCIPLE:** EQAO assessments are curriculum-based. Nothing on an assessment should require knowledge or skills beyond what can reasonably be related to curriculum expectations up to and including the grade of the assessment. (OSSLT – up to and including Grade 9)

1 AGE AND GRADE APPROPRIATE
- uses vocabulary and sentence structures appropriate to age and grade
- keeps wording of items as precise, simple and clear as possible
- ensures use of simple language for mathematic items so as not to hinder demonstration of mathematical knowledge and skill
- ensures materials are at an appropriate cognitive level to age and grade
- ensures materials are assessing reading, writing or mathematics expectations and not student knowledge of other curriculum subjects
- ensures material is accurate, current (up to date) and not likely to date before use

2 CURRICULUM LINKS
- uses vocabulary appropriate to the subject area or topic based on curriculum expectations up to and including the grade being assessed (OSSLT – up to and including Grade 9)
- uses common instructional phrases
- ensures items measure the skill, strategy or strand and expectation intended
- ensures items are coded to the most appropriate skill, strategy or strand and expectation for the grade assessed

3 STANDARD CANADIAN ENGLISH
- uses age- and grade-appropriate plain language
- uses standard Canadian spelling (first spelling in Oxford Canadian dictionary)
- limits unfamiliar words, idioms and idiomatic expressions

4 MULTIPLE-CHOICE ITEMS
- ensures items accurately link to the test specifications
- includes distractors based on common misconceptions and misunderstandings, and likely misreadings of the stimulus
- ensures all distractors are plausible and reasonable
- ensures each multiple-choice item has only one correct answer
- ensures student attention is not drawn to one option due to lack of parallelism (e.g., length, grammatical structure)
- ensures reading items do not force an interpretation on students
- ensures reading items measure reading comprehension and not a student's opinion

TABLE 11: Assessment Development Committee Considerations for Items (continued)

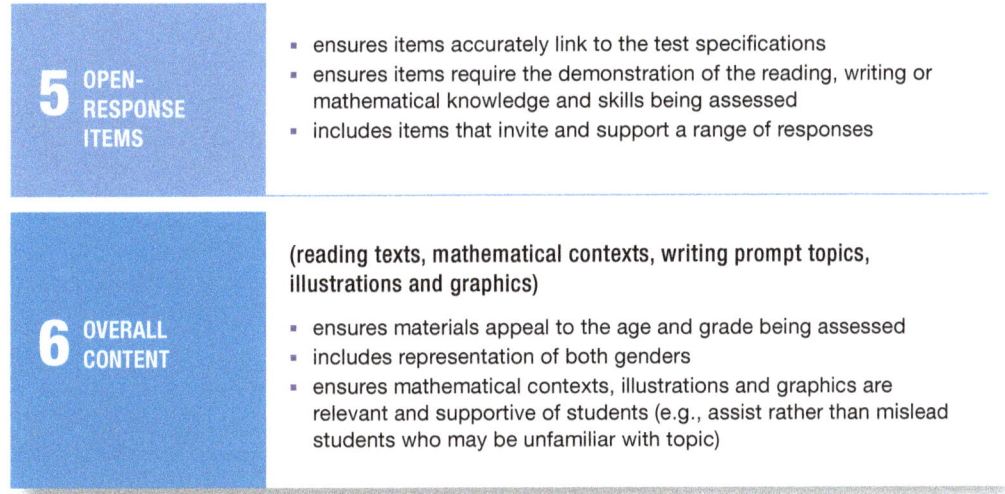

5	**OPEN-RESPONSE ITEMS**	<ul><li>ensures items accurately link to the test specifications</li><li>ensures items require the demonstration of the reading, writing or mathematical knowledge and skills being assessed</li><li>includes items that invite and support a range of responses</li></ul>
6	**OVERALL CONTENT**	(reading texts, mathematical contexts, writing prompt topics, illustrations and graphics)<ul><li>ensures materials appeal to the age and grade being assessed</li><li>includes representation of both genders</li><li>ensures mathematical contexts, illustrations and graphics are relevant and supportive of students (e.g., assist rather than mislead students who may be unfamiliar with topic)</li></ul>

Source: Adapted from EQAO Assessment Development Committee: Considerations for Items and Assessment Development – Review Considerations for Items, OSSLT; © by EQAO, used with permission.

Sensitivity Committee members are expected to possess

- expertise in and current experience with equity issues in education (e.g., multi-cultural, English- or French-language learners, students with special education needs) and
- expertise in and current experience with students and the curriculum in at least one of the grades being assessed.

The agency makes every effort to ensure Sensitivity Committee members represent an appropriate geographical and cultural cross-section of the province.

The Sensitivity Committees meet, under the supervision and guidance of EQAO staff, to provide feedback on the appropriateness of the reading selections and all of the language and mathematics assessment items. The main purpose of these committees' work is to ensure that assessment materials are free of bias and are as valid and as fair as possible for a wide range of students. Table 12 indicates the 10 elements that are considered by members of the Sensitivity Committee in their review of reading selections, multiple-choice items and writing prompts.

TABLE 12: Sensitivity Committee Considerations for Reading Selections and Items

GUIDING PRINCIPLE: Nothing on an assessment should cause a student to feel so upset, distracted or marginalized that he or she is unable to demonstrate the knowledge or skill being assessed.

1 UNIVERSALITY
- are appropriate for all participating students (including subpopulations of students)
- limits unfamiliar words, idioms and idiomatic expressions
- avoids language or phrases that may be objectionable to a particular group of students
- does not include materials that are inappropriate for English language learners (ELL) or students with disabilities

2 GENDER
- does not include themes, subject matter or organizational tone that favour one gender
- does not portray gender roles in a stereotypical or pejorative manner

3 GEOGRAPHY
- does not advantage or disadvantage students in certain parts of the province

4 SOCIO-ECONOMIC
- avoids inappropriate emphasis on wealth, poverty and crime
- does not suggest that affluence or poverty is attributed to a particular group
- does not suggest that belonging to a particular socio-economic group is more advantageous than another

5 SOCIAL AND ENVIRONMENTAL ISSUES
- does not include references to issues such as bullying, violence, gambling, addictions, criminal behaviour, homelessness
- avoids topics about family conflicts, birthdays and other specific celebrations
- Avoid focus on warfare, lives of soldiers (past or present).
- Avoid if focus is mainly on the decline, endangerment or extinction of current species, or on environmental devastation and/or global warming.

6 RACE, ETHNICITY AND CULTURE
- does not portray ethnic groups in a pejorative or stereotypical manner
- does not include topics that suggest one culture is preferred or superior to another
- does not include cultural iconographic references to celebrations, national holidays (other than Canadian), contests/prizes, imperial/metric conversion

TABLE 12: Sensitivity Committee Considerations for Reading Selections and Items (continued)

7 RELIGION	▪ avoids topics that require a student to assume a position that may be contrary to religious beliefs or teaching ▪ avoids religious references ▪ avoids references to magic, supernatural, mythology, witchcraft
8 DISABILITY	▪ includes people with disabilities in a natural and authentic manner ▪ does not portray disability or assumptions about a person's perceived challenges as a focus
9 AGE	▪ does not portray an age group in a stereotypical or pejorative manner ▪ does not portray one age group as more favourable than another
10 ANIMALS	▪ avoids references that suggest animals are expendable ▪ does not imply that keeping pets is a universal practice

SPECIFIC TOPICS TO AVOID		
	▪ Birthdays ▪ Cultural celebrations ▪ Politics ▪ Negative attitudes ▪ Death and dying ▪ Socio-economic status ▪ Houses as preferred dwellings ▪ Family structure ▪ Gender issues ▪ Sexual orientation	▪ Ethnicity or race ▪ Prizes and contests ▪ Gambling ▪ Pets ▪ Food restricted by certain religions ▪ Religion ▪ Unfamiliar topics (too difficult or culturally/historically exclusionary)

Source: Adapted from EQAO Sensitivity Committee: Review Considerations for Reading Selections; © *by EQAO, used with permission.*

The Assessment Development and Sensitivity Committee members recommend which items should be accepted without change, accepted with changes, or rejected. EQAO's Program Managers and education officers consider this information in developing the final drafts of these items. At this point the items are ready for field testing.

SUMMARY

This chapter describes three approaches to developing test items for large-scale assessment instruments and focuses primarily on the methods EQAO has adopted over time. The test blueprint which must be consistent with the purpose(s) of the assessment and aligned with the relevant curriculum expectations (content standards) provides all-important specifications that drive item development. Although testing professionals have important roles to play, the involvement of educators at key stages of test design and item development is crucial to an effective assessment program. Ethical considerations, including but not limited to universal design, permeate all aspects of test design and item development.

CHAPTER FOUR

FIELD TESTING AND ITEM SELECTION

FIELD TESTING MULTIPLE-CHOICE AND OPEN-RESPONSE ITEMS THAT REQUIRE A SHORT RESPONSE

Field testing assessment items with samples of students that represent the population of students provides data that can guide item selection for a subsequent assessment. The items may be field tested in forms external to the assessment instrument, added as a block of items at the end of an operational assessment instrument for the current year, or embedded within the operational assessment instrument for the current year. Regardless of the approach, the field-test items should not contribute to student scores.

The advantages of embedding the items within the operational assessment instrument are as follows:

- Since the students do not know what items are the embedded items and what items are the operational items, the concern of the lack of motivation that may occur among students when items are field tested in recognizable blocks within a test or are administered in separate field-test booklets outside of the regular assessment is addressed.

- If some or all of the field-test items that are identified as acceptable based on field-test results are included in a subsequent assessment, then they can be used in statistical/psychometric analysis work to equate the current assessment form with the subsequent assessment form.

With the exception of the writing prompts that require an extended response on the Primary and Junior assessments and the OSSLT, EQAO field tests all of the newly developed items as embedded items in the operational assessment for the year. Many jurisdictions do not embed writing prompts that require extended responses. The reason is that there are only one or two prompts that require an extended response. Given the small number, these prompts are easily remembered, resulting in the likelihood that the security of these prompts may be compromised. In addition, field testing prompts with an extended response would result in a significant amount of additional testing time with items that do not count toward the students' final score. For these reasons, EQAO does not field test the writing prompts that require an extended response by embedding them in an assessment. Instead, EQAO relies on field trials, which are described in the following section.

EQAO uses a matrix sample design to embed field-test items in fixed locations in each operational test form. The number of field-test items in each form is such that no more than 20% of a student's time on the assessment is taken up by them. Consequently, there are many forms, each with the same operational items for the current year, and a set of field-test items. For example, approximately 24 forms are prepared for the English-language OSSLT. Since the number of students in the French-language population in the province is much smaller than the number of students in the English-language population, there are about 12 forms. It follows, then, that there are more new field-tested items to consider for the next year's English-language OSSLT operational form than for next year's French-language OSSLT operational form.

The existence of populations with small numbers of students like the French-language OSSLT population illustrates the challenges in building operational forms for smaller student populations. One way to address this challenge is to move to field testing new items external to the current assessment. However, the issue of lack of student motivation would need to be accounted for.

OPEN-RESPONSE ITEMS THAT REQUIRE AN EXTENDED RESPONSE

Although, as mentioned above, EQAO does not formally field test writing prompts that require an extended response, it does conduct "field trials." The main purpose of the field trials is to confirm that the prompts are clear, engage students and result in a range of student responses that can be successfully (validly and reliably) scored. A purposeful but representative sample of schools is selected from across the province. Efforts are made to involve different schools and school boards each year. The number of schools involved is determined by the number of prompts and the number of students available to participate in the selected schools. The field trials also include a questionnaire for teachers that focusses on item quality and appropriateness. This questionnaire also includes questions the teachers pose to the students after they have completed the field trial. A copy of this questionnaire is provided in Table 13. Care is taken to ensure that writing prompts do not appear on an operational test the year after field trials to ensure that students of schools involved in the field trials will not be advantaged.

TABLE 13: Sample Teacher Questionnaire for Long-Writing Prompt Field Trials

OSSLT LONG WRITING FIELD-TRIAL QUESTIONNAIRE

Please complete one form for each classroom participating in the field trial.

School's name: _____

Teacher's name: _____

Program: [ ] Applied [ ] Academic [ ] Other

Prompt identification number (on cover page): _____

Post-Field-Trial Questions for Discussion with Students:

a. What did you think about or consider before you began to write?
b. Did this topic interest you? Why or why not?
c. Did you have enough ideas in order to respond to the prompt?
d. What did you like or not like about the prompt?

Summary of general comments from students:

_____
_____
_____
_____

Please circle the appropriate response. (1 = Strongly disagree, 4 = Strongly agree)

1. This prompt is understandable and of interest to a wide variety of students.   1 2 3 4
2. The students have enough related life experience to respond in a substantial way to this prompt.   1 2 3 4
3. Both male and female students can respond equally well to this prompt.   1 2 3 4
4. Nothing in this prompt would distress or offend students.   Yes   No

Other comments:

_____
_____
_____
_____

Thank you for your participation.

Source: Adapted from EQAO OSSLT Long Writing Field-Trial Questionnaire; © by EQAO, used with permission.

EQAO does not conduct a formal scoring of students' field-trial responses. Instead, educators, under the supervision of EQAO staff, read and sort responses according to whether they are deemed to be high-, medium- or low-level responses to the prompts (Grade 9 and OSSLT). Primary and Junior field-trial responses are sorted by codes 10, 20, 30 and 40. Like all EQAO reading selections and test items, the long-writing prompts are reviewed by the Assessment Development and Sensitivity Committees.

ITEM SELECTION OF MULTIPLE-CHOICE AND OPEN-RESPONSE ITEMS THAT REQUIRE A SHORT RESPONSE

Ideally, in large-scale assessment programs, items that are selected to become part of an operational test have been field tested in previous assessments. Item statistics must indicate the items are of high quality, fair for students and comparable to those on previous assessments. The field-tested multiple-choice and open-response items that require a short response are scored at the same time the operational items are scored. In large-scale assessments, field-test items are selected to become part of an operational test if, based on the analysis of the field-test responses, they have acceptable psychometric properties and they properly represent the domain to be assessed.

First, classical test theory (CTT) item statistics and/or item response theory (IRT) statistics are generated to analyze the field-test items and select items for an operational form. Differential item functioning (DIF) analyses are also conducted to determine if there are any items displaying potential bias either advantaging or disadvantaging certain groups of students.

Typically, large-scale assessment agencies initially employ CTT statistics – the difficulty expressed as the p-value (proportion of students who selected the correct option) and discrimination expressed as the point-biserial or, if the sample sizes are small, the corrected point-biserial – for each option of a multiple-choice item. These item statistics are for norm-referenced tests and are appropriate for criterion-referenced tests that assess thinking above the knowledge level, which will produce enough variation among the students' responses to make the interpretation of a point-biserial coefficient meaningful. The distribution of responses across score codes of a scoring rubric, the frequency of blank or no response rates, mean performance, correlation between item and the total test, and point-polyserial correlation (Olsson, Drasgow & Dorans, 1982) are typically used for the open-response items. The result of these analyses is a set of potential items for selection for the operational form the following year.

Difficulty and Discrimination

The criteria typically used in large-scale assessment using the CTT mean and point-biserial for multiple-choice items are as follows:

- For the correct option, p-value greater than or equal to 0.20 and point-biserial correlations greater than 0.20
- For the incorrect options, a negative point-biserial coefficient

For the open-response items, the criteria are as follows:

- Percent of students within each score code should progress from lower percentages of students in the lower codes and higher percentages in the higher codes of the scoring rubric
- Positive item-total correlation
- Point-polyserial correlations that progressively increase from negative values for the lower codes to positive values for the higher codes of the scoring rubric

Generally speaking, test items with p-values below 0.30 are considered relatively difficult, and test items with p-values above 0.80 are considered relatively easy.

Item response theory analyses are typically used to make the final selection of items for the operational form. These include item information functions for each potential multiple-choice item and for each score code for each potential open-response item, passage information functions for reading, and the test information function for each potential operational form. The operational form with the greatest amount of information is selected. Items not selected are placed in an item bank for future use. Indeed, when developing the operational form, it is often the case that one or two items from the current item bank are brought forward to the final form.

To illustrate the use of item statistics in item selection, consider the statistics for Primary reading reported in Table 14 for a sample of 22 field-tested multiple-choice items and in Table 15 for a sample of 18 field-tested open-response items. Given the field-test items were embedded in the operational forms, the point-biserial correlations for the multiple-choice items and the correlations and the point-polyserial correlations for the open-response items were computed using the total score on the operational form in which each field-test item was located.

As shown in Table 14, the difficulty of the multiple-choice items varied from 0.32 (item 14) to 0.97 (item 19). Taken together as a set, all but four of the items have difficulty indices greater than 0.60, and six items (6, 8, 9, 12, 13 and 19) have p-values greater than 0.90. For these items, either the students know well what is being asked for, the items are susceptible to test-wiseness or the distractors do not draw many students. It is usually desirable to have some easy items, but given the need to classify the students into four achievement levels, an appropriate balance of item difficulties is needed.

While three of the 22 sample multiple-choice items (3, 16 and 22) have point-biserials below 0.20 for the keyed or correct response, the point-biserials of the distractors are all negative. Careful examination of these 3 items is required to determine whether they are candidates for revision and re-field testing, or whether they should be rejected.

Turning to the sample of 18 open-response items that require a short response (Table 15), the first thing to note is that the rate of blank or no response is somewhat higher for the open-response than for the multiple-choice items. This is to be expected, since students are more apt to make a selection (or guess) than to write a response, if they are not sure of

TABLE 14: Field Test Multiple-Choice Item Analysis Statistics
Assessments of Reading, Writing and Mathematics — Grade 3 Reading (English Language)

Item Number	Overall Expectation Code	Key	Total N-Counts	Difficulty (p-value)	Answer Key Pbis	Option 1 Distractor 1	Option 2 Distractor 2	Option 3 Distractor 3	Option 4 Distractor 4	Blank (-9) N-Count	Blank (-9) Percent (%)
1	R1.0	3	8292	87.87	0.38	−0.23	−0.21		−0.19	11	0.13
2	R2.0	2	8292	74.47	0.39	−0.27		−0.19	−0.20	22	0.27
3	R2.0	4	8292	50.24	0.18	−0.03	−0.15	−0.08		46	0.55
4	R2.0	3	8292	43.10	0.25	−0.04	−0.24		−0.12	89	1.07
5	R1.0	4	6014	80.21	0.38	−0.18	−0.27	−0.21		10	0.17
6	R1.0	1	6014	94.78	0.27		−0.14	−0.19	−0.14	9	0.15
7	R1.0	4	6014	86.10	0.40	−0.30	−0.14	−0.19		12	0.20
8	R1.0	4	6014	90.72	0.35	−0.23	−0.14	−0.21		15	0.25
9	R1.0	3	6014	93.03	0.35	−0.23	−0.20		−0.17	12	0.20
10	R1.0	3	6014	72.93	0.48	−0.24	−0.31		−0.18	23	0.38
11	R1.0	1	6014	83.75	0.31		−0.19	−0.19	−0.14	6	0.10
12	R1.0	4	5902	90.78	0.44	−0.29	−0.22	−0.24		9	0.15
13	R1.0	2	5902	95.27	0.32	−0.17		−0.19	−0.19	9	0.15
14	R3.0	4	5902	31.84	0.33	−0.02	−0.20	−0.29		15	0.25
15	R1.0	2	5940	75.49	0.38	−0.27		−0.17	−0.19	21	0.35
16	R2.0	1	5940	85.07	0.19		−0.09	−0.11	−0.13	18	0.30
17	R1.0	4	5842	86.05	0.24	−0.23	−0.13	−0.10		4	0.07
18	R3.0	3	5842	88.36	0.36	−0.20	−0.08		−0.26	11	0.19
19	R2.0	1	6011	96.87	0.23		−0.17	−0.12	−0.12	5	0.08
20	R1.0	4	6011	54.77	0.27	−0.25	−0.24	−0.01		3	0.05
21	R2.0	2	5935	77.46	0.31	−0.29		−0.12	−0.08	25	0.42
22	R2.0	1	5859	81.74	0.11		−0.11	−0.06	−0.06	12	0.20

Frequency Distribution										
Ambiguous (-6)		Option 1		Option 2		Option 3		Option 4		
N-Count	Percent (%)	N-Count	Percent (%)	N-Count	Percent (%)	N-Count	Percent (%)	N-Count	Percent (%)	Percent (%)
1	0.01	483	5.82	390	4.70	7286	87.87	121	1.46	100
2	0.02	486	5.86	6175	74.47	1304	15.73	303	3.65	100
4	0.05	2178	26.27	713	8.60	1185	14.29	4166	50.24	100
3	0.04	1654	19.95	352	4.25	3574	43.10	2620	31.60	100
		86	1.43	317	5.27	777	12.92	4824	80.21	100
1	0.02	5700	94.78	34	0.57	188	3.13	82	1.36	100
2	0.03	385	6.40	68	1.13	369	6.14	5178	86.10	100
		331	5.50	68	1.13	144	2.39	5456	90.72	100
2	0.03	124	2.06	226	3.76	5595	93.03	55	0.91	100
1	0.02	508	8.45	936	15.56	4386	72.93	160	2.66	100
		5037	83.75	658	10.94	236	3.92	77	1.28	100
		234	3.96	84	1.42	217	3.68	5358	90.78	100
		97	1.64	5623	95.27	84	1.42	89	1.51	100
3	0.05	2931	49.66	470	7.96	604	10.23	1879	31.84	100
		580	9.76	4484	75.49	74	1.25	781	13.15	100
1	0.02	5053	85.07	599	10.08	168	2.83	101	1.70	100
3	0.05	110	1.88	154	2.64	544	9.31	5027	86.05	100
2	0.03	242	4.14	63	1.08	5162	88.36	362	6.20	100
		5823	96.87	44	0.73	90	1.50	49	0.82	100
1	0.02	1033	17.19	167	2.78	1515	25.20	3292	54.77	100
		706	11.90	4597	77.46	81	1.36	526	8.86	100
		4789	81.74	85	1.45	767	13.09	206	3.52	100

Source: Adapted from EQAO records; © by EQAO, used with permission.

TABLE 15: Field Test Open-Response Item Analysis Statistics
Assessments of Reading, Writing and Mathematics — Grade 3 Reading (English Language)

Item Number	Overall Expectation Code	Max Score Code	N-Count	Difficulty (Average Performance as %)	Pbis	Polyserial Correlation				No Response (-9)	
						Code 10	Code 20	Code 30	Code 40	N-Count	Percent (%)
1	R1.0	4	1303	59.44	0.45	−0.31	−0.13	0.22	0.26		
2	R1.0	4	1303	48.45	0.44	−0.35	0.04	0.18	0.30	7	0.54
3	R1.0	4	1275	60.78	0.30	−0.21	−0.04	0.09	0.15	1	0.08
4	R1.0	4	1331	54.55	0.37	−0.31	0.00	0.17	0.21	5	0.38
5	R1.0	4	1294	49.09	0.34	−0.28	−0.04	0.20	0.25	10	0.77
6	R1.0	4	1336	54.00	0.42	−0.28	−0.04	0.22	0.21		
7	R1.0	4	1336	53.01	0.40	−0.26	−0.07	0.25	0.19	3	0.22
8	R1.0	4	1363	66.95	0.44	−0.28	−0.24	0.10	0.35		
9	R1.0	4	1363	50.86	0.42	−0.32	−0.03	0.21	0.25	10	0.73
10	R1.0	4	1304	52.63	0.39	−0.32	−0.01	0.18	0.26	2	0.15
11	R1.0	4	1314	49.83	0.40	−0.25	−0.05	0.17	0.29	6	0.46
12	R1.0	4	1314	56.62	0.39	−0.26	−0.05	0.15	0.23	5	0.38
13	R1.0	4	1363	48.77	0.39	−0.30	−0.06	0.27	0.24	5	0.37
14	R2.0	4	1363	29.33	0.36	−0.28	0.13	0.26	0.20	11	0.81
15	R1.0	4	1288	40.68	0.43	−0.30	−0.01	0.25	0.29	20	1.55
16	R1.0	4	1224	62.60	0.47	−0.34	−0.12	0.18	0.28		
17	R1.0	4	1304	46.13	0.29	−0.28	0.02	0.17	0.23	4	0.31
18	R2.0	4	1278	74.80	0.41	−0.29	−0.17	−0.03	0.35	1	0.08

Frequency Distribution										
Unengaged (-8)		Code 10		Code 20		Code 30		Code 40		
N-Count	Percent (%)	N-Count	Percent (%)	N-Count	Percent (%)	N-Count	Percent (%)	N-Count	Percent (%)	Percent (%)
25	1.92	164	12.59	407	31.24	508	38.99	199	15.27	100
35	2.69	346	26.55	417	32.00	304	23.33	194	14.89	100
3	0.24	101	7.92	628	49.25	392	30.75	150	11.76	100
13	0.98	225	16.90	577	43.35	370	27.80	141	10.59	100
31	2.40	265	20.48	484	37.40	370	28.59	134	10.36	100
26	1.95	228	17.07	500	37.43	462	34.58	120	8.98	100
23	1.72	203	15.19	570	42.66	447	33.46	90	6.74	100
36	2.64	73	5.36	295	21.64	561	41.16	398	29.20	100
45	3.30	235	17.24	448	32.87	408	29.93	217	15.92	100
25	1.92	253	19.40	528	40.49	330	25.31	166	12.73	100
22	1.67	436	33.18	324	24.66	339	25.80	187	14.23	100
15	1.14	195	14.84	492	37.44	466	35.46	141	10.73	100
29	2.13	226	16.58	682	50.04	338	24.80	83	6.09	100
88	6.46	480	35.22	482	35.36	250	18.34	52	3.82	100
56	4.35	360	27.95	345	26.79	354	27.48	153	11.88	100
20	1.63	161	13.15	311	25.41	488	39.71	246	20.10	100
31	2.38	417	31.98	392	30.06	351	26.92	109	8.36	100
16	1.25	89	6.96	252	19.72	312	24.41	608	47.57	100

Source: Adapted from EQAO records; © by EQAO, used with permission.

the correct answer. The difficulty of these items varied from 29% (Item 14) to 75% (Item 18). Interestingly, the rates of no response and unengaged are relatively high for Item 14, suggesting that this item may need to be revised and re-field tested or discarded.

The correlations between the item and the score on the operational items ranged from 0.29 (item 17) to 0.47 (Item 16). The polyserial correlations generally increased from Code 10 to Code 40. Generally it is expected that the percentage of students who receive at least Code 30 will be greater than the percentage of students who do not. The frequency distribution indicated that this happened for only four items (1, 8, 16 and 18). Of the remaining 14 items, the percentage of students at Code 20 was greater than the percentage of students at Code 10 for most of the items; for item 11, the percentage of students who received a Code 20 was smaller than for Code 10. For the remaining three items (14, 15 and 17) the percentages were about equal. At a minimum, these four items would be reviewed to determine if the scoring rubrics need to be refined.

Differential Item Functioning (DIF)

One goal of test development is to assemble a set of items that provides an estimate of a student's ability that is as fair and as accurate as possible for all groups within the population. Differential item functioning (DIF) statistics are used to identify items on which students with the same level of ability but from different identifiable groups have different probabilities of answering correctly (e.g., females and males, African Americans, Hispanics). Standard 7.3 of the *Standards for Educational and Psychological Testing* (1999) calls for DIF analysis. If an item is more difficult for one subgroup than another, then the reason may be due to the item itself, or the item may be measuring something different from the intended construct. However, it is important to recognize that DIF-flagged items might be related to actual differences in relevant knowledge or skill. If the reason is the first of these two mentioned above, then the item is said to be biased. If the reason is the second of the two mentioned, then the difference is said to be the result of item impact. Biased items should be examined and revised or discarded from the pool of potential field-test items.

Different classification systems have been developed for multiple-choice (Roussos & Stout, 1996) and open-response (Gierl & Bolt, 2001) items for identifying whether the difference observed is significant or not and, if significant, how large the significance is. Generally, three classes are formed:

- Items considered to have negligible DIF are classified as A.
- Items considered to have moderate amounts of DIF are classified as B.
- Items considered to have a large amount of DIF are classified as C.

Items classified as B or C should be reviewed by content experts, bias/sensitivity committees and, if possible, using think-aloud protocols followed by protocol analysis (Ericsson & Simon, 1993) to determine possible sources and interpretations of the differences.

EQAO examined the 2011-2012 assessments for gender- and second-language-learner-based (SLL based) DIF using the Mantel-Haenszel (MH) procedure (Mantel & Haenszel, 1959) for multiple-choice items and Mantel's (1963) extension of the MH procedure, in conjunction with the standardized mean difference (SMD) (Dorans, 1989), for open-response items. In the Primary- and Junior-Division assessments, 19 of the 344 items indicated gender-based DIF (17 B-level and two C-level). Among these items, 15 multiple-choice items favoured the boys and one favoured the girls; the three open-response items favoured the girls. These items were reviewed by the Assessment Team's education officers and content experts, and no apparent biases were identified in the content of the items (Education Quality and Accountability Office, 2013b). The differential performance between females and males may have been the result of item impact. Due to various constraints, protocol analyses (similar to cognitive labs) were not conducted but could have been useful in understanding more fully the reasons for DIF.

TEST FORM CONSTRUCTION

Test agencies use the results of the classical item analyses presented above to create a set of potential items for the operational form for the following year. The final set of items is selected using IRT. Item information functions for each item in the pool of potential items, passage information functions for the reading selections in the pool of potential items, and the target test information function for each potential set of items for each subject, grade and language group are developed. The final set of items for an operational test form is the set that best fits the target test information function for the subject and grade level, subject to the condition that the final set of items represents the domain for the subject and grade level assessed, and its difficulty is close to the average difficulty for the previous three years. It is important that each test contains the right mix of items that reflects the measureable learning expectations (subject content, thinking skills) and item difficulties for each assessment year. At the same time, it is important to have maximum information which in turn will lead to small error of measurement. The selection of items and the creation of an appropriate test form for the subject area and age of students, therefore, involve both science (data) and art (professional judgment) components.

Consequently, the selection of EQAO's operational test forms involves the close collaboration of the education officers and the psychometricians. This involves a back-and-forth process in which the education officers select items based on the item statistics in light of the curriculum and test blueprint; the psychometricians pay particular attention to the statistical properties of the items and test forms and the fit to the target test information function. Once the education officers make a preliminary selection of items for the proposed test forms, the psychometricians produce the test difficulty, reliability and the test information function for the provisional test. Through an interactive process in which items are replaced with other items in the pool, subject to domain representation, a final operational test form is constructed with a test information function that best fits the target information function. Further, since field-test items from the previous year are selected as operational items for the following year, the operational form for next year and the operational form for the current year can be equated to provide a measure of change.

Addition of Open-response Items that Require an Extended Response

At this point the open-response items that require an extended response are added to the operational forms. EQAO does not conduct a formal scoring of students' field-trial responses. Instead, educators, under the supervision of EQAO staff, read and sort responses according to whether they are deemed to be high-, medium- or low-level responses to the prompts (or sorted by codes 10, 20, 30 and 40 in the case of the Primary and Junior assessments). Items for which there is not an "even" distribution are revised and re-trialled or rejected. The remaining items are reviewed by the Assessment Development and Sensitivity Committees. Items approved by these committees are then considered by the education officers and content experts, and the desired number is selected. The selection is made from items trialled two or more years prior to the year of the present assessment year to avoid an unfair advantage for students and schools in which the item was tried out and considering the item(s) included in the previous year's assessment and the content of reading selections in the new operational form to avoid overlap.

Review by Psychometric Panel

The recommended operational test forms with open-response items that require an extended response in both English and French are taken to the agency's Psychometric Expert Panel (PEP) for validation. EQAO's PEP (referred to as a Technical Advisory Committee or TAC in some jurisdictions) usually has about seven Canadian and American testing and measurement experts. The PEP meets two to three times a year to validate the test forms for the up-coming year with respect to the conditions for equating and to provide advice as requested by the agency on a range of large-scale assessment issues. The meeting dates are selected to allow time to make any changes that might be recommended and, importantly, to prepare, print, and distribute the operational forms prior to the administration dates.

The information considered by PEP with respect to equating includes the following:

- Minimum, maximum, mean, and standard deviation of multiple-choice items and the open-response items that require a short response for the previous year's assessments and the estimated values based on the analyses of the field-test multiple-choice and open-response items that require a short answer proposed for inclusion in the current year's assessments

- Average test difficulty for the previous three years and last year and the estimated difficulty for the current year; distribution of item-total correlations and difficulty for the field-test items selected for the current year

- Test characteristic curve for last year and estimated for the current year; test information function for last year and estimated for the current year, together with the target information function for the reading and mathematics assessments

- Test characteristic curve and test information function for the previous year and estimated for the current year, excluding the open-response items that require an extended response and including the open-response item(s) that require an extended response, where the extended-response item(s) for the previous year are included in the current year's assessments for writing and the OSSLT

- Classical and item response theory difficulty and discrimination values for the field-test items to be included in the current year's operational form

ITEM BANKING

Some large-scale assessment programs develop only the required number and type of items that are needed for an up-coming assessment, taking into consideration the development of extra items to allow for those that are rejected, as described earlier. Most large-scale assessment programs, however, have their own electronic item banks or have access to them through a contractor.

Electronic item banks are particularly valuable where multiple operational forms of an assessment are produced. For example, multiple forms would be required in a test-on-demand situation in which students can write the test when they are ready and not all at the same time. Electronic item banks are also needed when computer adaptive testing is used. With the right setup and security arrangements, the development of items can be conducted within the item bank. When item development takes place outside an item bank, the items can be imported into the bank following their development. In either case, being able to work on items electronically within a bank is much more efficient than manually manipulating them. In addition, when items are in final form, the required operational test forms can be generated directly out of an item bank.

QUESTIONNAIRES

Student achievement results on large-scale assessments provide important information about educational quality. However, these results can only be interpreted meaningfully if there is contextual information about the education system that produced them. Most large-scale assessment programs, therefore, include questionnaires to gather contextual data that can be reported alongside achievement results. The principal purposes for gathering contextual data are three-fold:

- To provide demographic and other education-related environmental information that will help teachers, administrators and the public interpret student achievement results in the context of the school, school board and province

- To provide information that can be used by decision-makers at the school, board and provincial levels for improvement planning

- To encourage research that will result in useful information to effect change that will improve student learning

EQAO enhances its reporting of achievement results by including demographic data and information about school environments that can be used to interpret student achievement results in context. For each of its assessments, EQAO gathers contextual data through a Student Data Collection system (SDC) in which school and school board data are uploaded directly from board data collection systems. In addition, the agency administers student, teacher and principal questionnaires (Primary and Junior assessments); student and teacher questionnaires (Grade 9 assessment) and student questionnaires (OSSLT) which are completed during the period of the assessments. In designing its questionnaires, agency staff reviews the literature and practices in other jurisdictions and testing organizations on an ongoing basis.

To elaborate further on the content of questionnaires, and by way of an example, EQAO collects and reports on the following types of information related to the Primary and Junior Assessments of Reading, Writing and Mathematics:

For Students

- Student characteristics (e.g., age, language spoken)
- Attitudes toward reading, writing and mathematics
- Perception of their performance in reading, writing and mathematics
- Use of technology at home and school
- Home support for learning

For Teachers

- Classroom characteristics
- Access to and use of resources for teaching and assessment of reading, writing and mathematics
- Teacher collaboration
- Use of EQAO data and resources
- Teacher information (e.g., background, experience, qualifications, professional development)

For Principals

- School characteristics
- Student attendance
- Human resources (e.g., staffing and staff support)
- Communication with parents
- Use of EQAO data and resources
- School improvement planning
- Principal information (e.g., background, experience, qualifications, professional development)

More information about the agency's questionnaires can be found on the EQAO Web site.

SUMMARY

The foregoing discussions illustrate that the item and test development process is a lengthy one. In year one, the items are developed, and the best among them are selected for field testing in year two. Following field testing, the best items are selected for the operational assessment in year three. If the development and/or identification of reading selections is taken into consideration in this timetable, the item and test development process takes at least three full years for test materials to be developed and to eventually find their way onto operational test forms.

Regular and systematic reflection on and revision to (where necessary) aspects of the assessment program, including the item and test development processes, should be institutionalized in large-scale assessment, for as Redfield (2001) states

> ...test development is a dynamic, long-term process requiring periodic review and revision.... (pp. 62-63)

CHAPTER FIVE

TEST ADMINISTRATION

ETHICAL CONSIDERATIONS

In keeping with the *Principles for Fair Student Assessment Practices for Education in Canada,* those directly impacted by the assessment (students, parents/guardians, educators) should be provided with complete information about how the students will be assessed. Test developers or testing organizations, therefore, should develop materials and procedures for informing test users[2] about test instructions, the content of the assessment, the number and types of questions being used, samples of test items examples of what constitutes complete responses to the items and the procedures to follow to appeal a result, especially for high-stakes tests.

---

[2] *"Test users" is used in the broadest way here to include test takers/students, invigilators, educators, parents/guardians and the public – anyone who has an interest in the assessment and its results.*

To students with special education needs and students who are not yet proficient in the language of instruction to respond to the assessment, information about the types of accommodations available for students who use these accommodations through the school year on a regular basis and, if allowed, alternative forms for students who cannot respond to the assessment as administered, should be provided to users (*Principles for Fair Student Assessment Practices for Education in Canada,* 1993). Likewise information should be provided to users in jurisdictions in which alternatives are provided to the assessment, such as taking a course. In addition, information should be provided to help students and their parents/guardians decide whether or not to participate in an assessment in cases where participation is optional.

Clear and appropriate instructions must be provided for students, teachers, principals and others involved in test administration to ensure the assessment is administered consistently across the jurisdiction and to ensure fairness for all students who need to know what is required of them.

Sufficient lead time (i.e., at least one year) should be provided to students and educators prior to implementing major changes to a testing program, particularly in the case of high-stakes assessment.

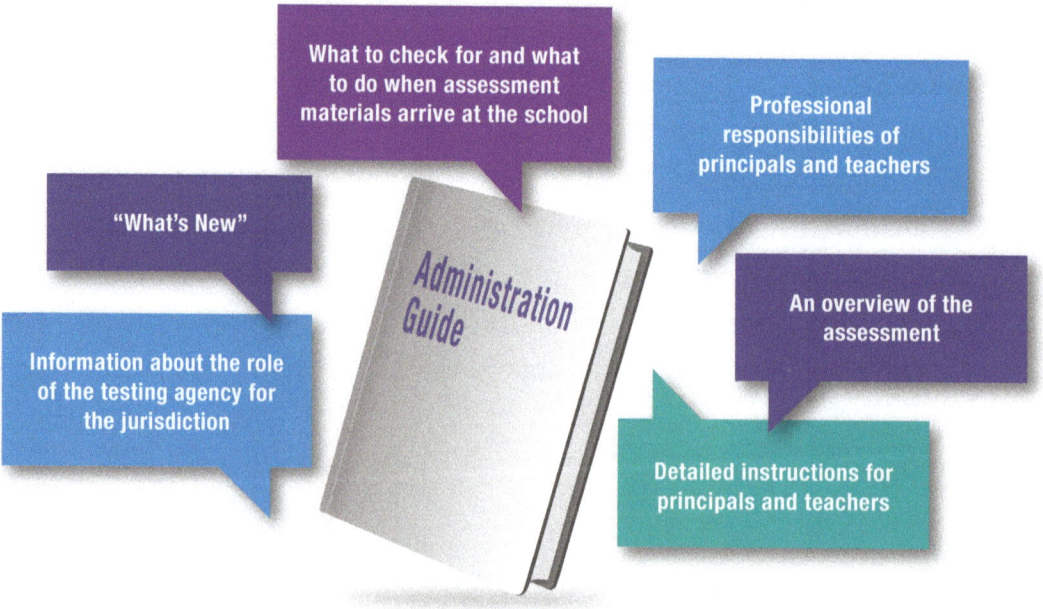

ADMINISTRATION GUIDES

Administration guides provide detailed descriptions of the test administration procedures teachers and principals must follow and what their professional responsibilities are with respect to test administration. In jurisdictions with multiple languages of instruction, separate administration guides for each language group should be developed, and copies should be sent to each school administering the given assessment. EQAO administration guides (2014) are typically 10 to 12 pages in length and provide the following types of information:

- A "What's New" section at the beginning of the document (Since most of the administration procedures remain consistent from year-to-year, it is important to highlight any administrative changes, if any, for the current year.)
- What to check for and what to do when assessment materials arrive at the school, perhaps in the form of a checklist, to ensure that all the materials have been received by each school and a second checklist to ensure that the school returns the correct materials to the testing agency
- Professional responsibilities of principals and teachers, including what teachers and principals need to do before, during and after the assessment and what they are not to do before (e.g., look at the test and then teach their students; copy the test), during (e.g., provide assistance to students such as discussing an item with which the students appear to be having difficulty or providing an outline for the open-response items that require an extended response) and after the assessment (e.g., change students' answers)
- An overview of the assessment, including a description of the student booklets that comprise the assessment and the administration schedule
- Detailed instructions for principals and teachers to ensure the consistent administration of the assessment across the jurisdiction

- Information about the role of the testing agency for the jurisdiction (brief description of the agency's policies and procedures for item development, scoring and reporting)

ACCOMMODATIONS

Accommodations are supports and services that enable students with special education needs and students who are in the early stages of acquiring the language of the test to demonstrate their competencies in the skills being measured by the assessment. Accommodations change only the way in which the assessment is administered or the way in which a student responds to the components of the assessment. They do not alter the content of the assessment or affect the validity or reliability of the assessment results.

Special provisions are changes to the setting for writing the assessment, usually for English language learners. These provisions do not affect the validity or reliability of the assessment.

Modifications, on the other hand, are changes to content and to performance criteria. Modifications are generally not permitted in large-scale assessments because the scores of the students provided modifications cannot be validity interpreted in terms of the assessment results for the remaining students. Thus, students who would need modifications are often exempted from the assessment. Some jurisdictions (e.g., in the U.S.) provide alternate assessments for students who would otherwise require modifications.

DEFERRALS AND EXEMPTIONS

There are philosophical, legal and practical reasons for wishing to include all eligible students, including students who are in the early stages of learning the language of the test and students with special education needs, in large-scale assessments. There are instances, however, when students are unable to participate. For example, students may be exempted if they are unable to participate even with the allowable accommodations. Students may be deferred if they do not yet possess sufficient English- or French-language reading and writing proficiency to participate.

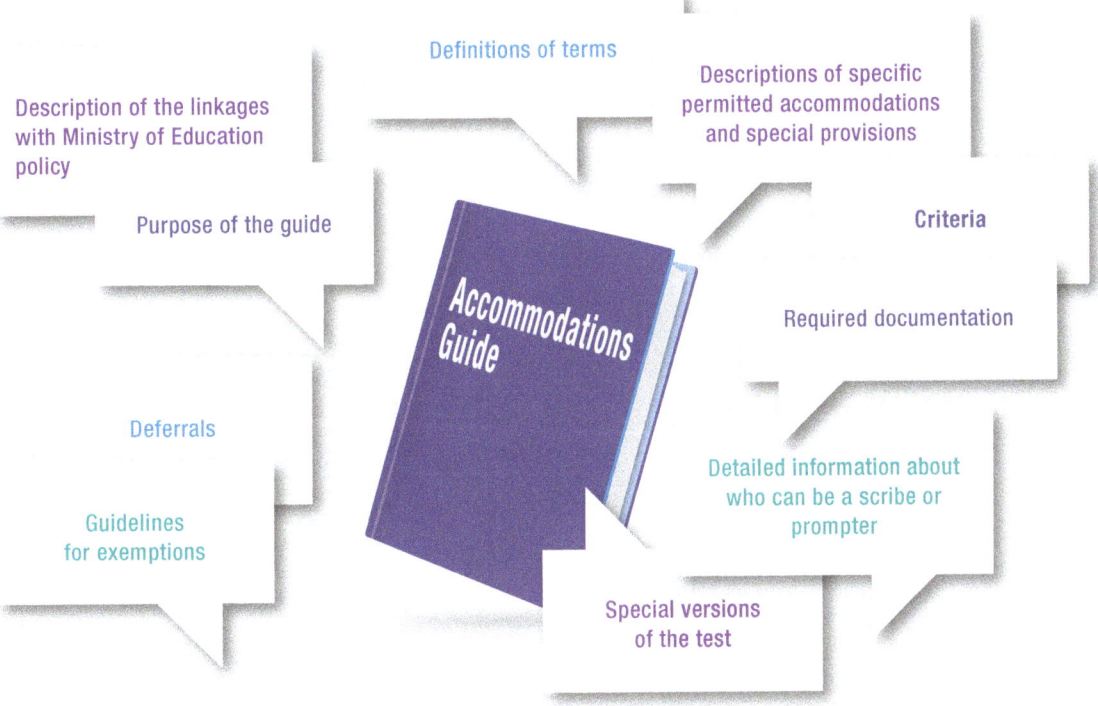

ACCOMMODATIONS GUIDES

Accommodations guides provide information to principals and teachers to help them make decisions about accommodations for students with special education needs and special provisions for second-language learners, students with special circumstances (e.g., a temporary hand/arm injury) and exemptions and deferrals where appropriate. For example, EQAO prepares guides for accommodations and special provisions for each of its assessments. These guides include the following types of information:

- Purpose of the guide
- Description of the linkages with Ministry of Education policy
- Definitions of terms (i.e., modifications, accommodations, special provisions, exemptions, deferrals)

- Descriptions of specific permitted accommodations and special provisions

- Criteria upon which to base the decision to permit accommodations, special provisions, deferrals and exemptions

- Required documentation for accommodations, special provisions, deferrals and exemptions (where appropriate, depending on the assessment)

- Detailed information about who can be a scribe or prompter and what a scribe or prompter may and may not do

- Special versions of the test (e.g., uncontracted and contracted Braille, large-print booklets, regular-print or large-print booklets on coloured paper [e.g., blue, green, yellow], MP3/audio CD with regular-print or large-print booklets) and forms of assistive technology (e.g., text-to-speech software or augmentative or alternative communications systems with regular-print booklets) which are available on EQAO's secure Web site 48 to 72 hours (depending on the assessment) prior to the start of the test

- Guidelines for exemptions (e.g., Grade 3 [Primary Division] and Grade 6 [Junior Division] may be exempted if they are unable to participate even with the allowable accommodations or special provisions. For the OSSLT, the only allowable exemption is if a student's Individual Education Plan (IEP) indicates he/she is not working toward an Ontario Secondary School Diploma (OSSD). No exemptions are permitted for the Grade 9 Mathematics Assessment. The rationale for this position is that if the student is registered in and working toward a credit in Grade 9 mathematics, then there is no reason why a student would not participate in the provincial assessment.

- Deferrals are only granted for the OSSLT. All Ontario students who are working toward an Ontario Secondary School Diploma are expected to write the OSSLT in Grade 10; however, a deferral can be granted in the following circumstances:

- The student does not yet possess sufficient English- or French-language reading and writing proficiency to participate.
- The student has been identified as having special education needs and is not able to participate even with the permitted accommodations.
- The student is new to the school board, requires accommodations, and the appropriate accommodations cannot be provided.

OTHER SUPPORTIVE DOCUMENTS AND RESOURCES

It is important to provide additional information to educators, students and parents/guardians beyond that which is found in the administration and accommodations guides. For example, providing released items from previous assessments, sample tests (where appropriate), scoring rubrics and samples of student work that demonstrate the expected quality of work required should be provided, so that teachers, students and parents have a good idea of what is expected.

In addition to the administration and accommodations guides, EQAO posts a wide range of resource material related to its assessments on its Web site at www.eqao.com. This information includes the following:

- Bulletins for teachers, students and parents/guardians that provide overviews of the assessments and administration procedures (in the case of the OSSLT, a description of the appeal process, is also provided)
- Previous assessment material with scoring rubrics and student responses at the various score codes
- School success stories (which will be expanded upon in the chapter on reporting)
- Instructional strategies for teachers (which will also be elaborated in the chapter on reporting)
- Sample individual student reports
- Links to other important resources such as the framework documents and technical reports

ADMINISTRATION SCHEDULE

Generally speaking, it is most desirable to administer curriculum-based assessments as close as possible to the end of the semester or school year, so that students have the benefit of as much instructional time as possible. Most jurisdictions take a variety of other elements into consideration as well, such as times when absenteeism might be high (e.g., inclement weather, major holidays) or the administration of the assessment in international schools (particularly for high-stakes tests) when deciding when to administer large-scale assessments. In addition, if reporting of student results is required before the end of the school year (e.g., for graduation purposes), then the timing of test administration will need to account for the time required for receiving of test materials, scoring of student work and data analysis.

For example, the EQAO Primary and Junior Assessments of Reading, Writing and Mathematics are administered annually in a two-week "window" of time toward the end of May and the beginning of June. As was mentioned earlier, the Primary and Junior assessments contain three booklets, each divided into two parts which require one hour. Thus, the Primary and Junior assessments are conducted in six one-hour time blocks. Scheduling is at the convenience of the school during the two week interval. The Grade 9 Mathematics Assessment is administered in January for first-semester students and in June for second-semester students and students taking full-year courses. Like the Primary and Junior assessments, the Grade 9 assessment is also administered in a two-week time window. Each of the two booklets is administered in a 60-minute time block, and scheduling is at the convenience of the school. The OSSLT is administered on a single morning toward the end of March or the beginning of April each year. The test is divided into two parts, each of which requires 75 minutes with a 15 minute break between the two parts. (The timing of the OSSLT administration is appropriate given the test is not based on the curriculum of a specific course but covers a range of cross-curricular reading and writing expectations up to the end of Grade 9.) The administration is kept to one morning in response to the scheduling needs of schools and to avoid unauthorized release of the assessment materials if the assessment was conducted over two days. Also, the OSSLT is administered in some international schools where students are working toward an Ontario Secondary School Diploma, since passing the OSSLT is a high school graduation requirement. Administration of the OSSLT in countries beyond the International Date Line (e.g., China and Malaysia) takes place on the day following the scheduled date for administration in Ontario (and therefore takes place at roughly the same time as in Ontario). Administration of the test in European countries, the Middle East and Africa is conducted on the same date and time as in Ontario. Taking time changes into account in this way means that the tests are administered at approximately the same time, thereby minimizing the risk of unauthorized release of test materials due to time zone differences.

DISTRIBUTION AND RECEIPT OF ASSESSMENT MATERIALS

Test agencies that use paper-and-pencil assessments need to develop procedures for the distribution and receipt of student assessment materials to and from the schools and for tracking purposes. Often the test material is delivered to and picked up from the schools by bonded contracted couriers to ensure that the test booklets arrive at the school, and the completed booklets arrive at the testing agency or a designated scoring center.

EQAO engages contractors to ship assessment materials to and from schools. Quality assurance procedures are documented to ensure that test materials are never left unattended during the delivery process. All test materials are returned to the agency; copying materials or retaining copies is not permitted. EQAO tracks the return of assessment materials from schools and follows up with them when necessary to ensure all materials have been accounted for.

ADMINISTRATION FORMATS

Although many large-scale assessment programs continue to provide the tests in paper-and-pen/pencil format, several jurisdictions/programs are offering or plan to offer student achievement tests in electronic format (e-assessments). At the international level, for example, the 2015 Programme for International Student Assessment (PISA) will be entirely computer-based (Organisation for Economic Co-operation and Development, 2013). In the U.S., many large-scale testing companies/vendors provide states with computer-based test administration services, and the Partnership for the Assessment of Readiness for College and Careers (PARCC) and Smarter Balanced consortiums plan to offer computer-based testing beginning in 2015 (PARCC and Smarter Balanced consortiums, 2013). In Canada, British Columbia's Foundation Skills Assessments in reading comprehension, writing and numeracy, administered to students in Grades 4 and 7, as well as many of the Grades 10 to 12 graduation examinations, administered to students in Grades 10, 11 and 12, are e-assessments (British Columbia Ministry of Education, 2013). In Alberta, the Ministry of Education plans to offer all diploma examinations in electronic format, together with an online digital marking system, by the fall of 2017 (Rickwood, 2013). In Ontario, EQAO's assessment program is currently paper-based; however, the agency has been conducting research and is planning to initiate image-based scoring and computer-based assessments beginning in 2015 and 2016, respectively.

QUALITY ASSURANCE IN TEST ADMINISTRATION

Students, educators, the public and the testing organization need to be confident that the results of the large-scale assessment are reliable and can be validly interpreted. It is important, therefore, that quality assurance measures are in place to demonstrate that the administration procedures have been implemented consistently across the jurisdiction. Most jurisdictions rely on their test instructions to provide for administration consistency and include instructions restricting advance access to the specific content of the test and about not copying the test booklets to ensure security. Some jurisdictions use computer software packages to analyze patterns of student responses to multiple-choice items for evidence of copying or sharing answers. Scorers of student responses to open-response items are instructed to look for different hand writing, a large number of erasures or corrections made in a different pen colour for evidence of cheating. It is important to implement sound quality assurance procedures, but once they are in place, the testing organization must be prepared to act on the information that surfaces. For instance, if computer analysis of student responses suggests that possible cheating has occurred, not acting on that information is likely to destroy confidence in the test results and may completely discredit the testing program. It is important that the testing organization have in place well-thought-out policies and detailed action plans that cover the various issues that can arise, such as inclement weather, administration irregularities and breaches of test security.

In addition to the administration procedures previously mentioned, including the provision of administration guides that provide detailed instructions for teachers and principals, EQAO has implemented four quality assurance procedures to help ensure that its assessments are administered consistently and fairly across the province.

Quality Assurance Monitors

EQAO contracts quality assurance monitors who visit a random sample of approximately five percent of schools to observe the administration of the assessments. The combined number of English- and French-language schools visited are 220 schools for the Primary and Junior assessments, 30 schools for the Grade 9 assessments and 35 schools for the OSSLT. The monitors prepare reports that detail the extent to which test administration procedures were followed before, during and after the assessment.

Internet and Social Media Monitoring

EQAO monitors the Internet and social media to gauge whether or not test security has been breached and the test items exposed. This monitoring takes place prior to, during and immediately after an assessment period for the Primary, Junior and Grade 9 assessments and prior to, during, and immediately after the administration of the OSSLT.

Pre-scoring Review of Test Materials

Another approach EQAO uses to look for any evidence of potential irregularities in test administration is the examination of test materials prior to scoring. During the process of receiving the test materials from schools, the agency's education officers review student booklets for approximately a five-percent random sample of schools. The students' work, including their open responses and machine-scorable forms (student answer sheets), are examined for unusual erasure patterns for multiple-choice items and common or identical wording and corrections in student responses to open-responses items.

Database Analyses

EQAO conducts two kinds of database analyses of student response data. The first involves a collusion analysis of responses to multiple-choice items that identifies student response patterns that suggest the possibility of cheating among students in a school or potentially across schools. When the collusion analysis indicates a perfect or near perfect pattern of incorrect and correct responses among students, EQAO contacts the school principal to request further information, and if necessary, to launch an investigation.

The second type of database analysis involves the examination of overall patterns of Primary, Junior and Grade 9 assessment school results over time and identifying unusually large improvements in the proportion of students who achieved the provincial standard (Level 3).

In the rare cases where administration irregularities are suspected or are directly reported to EQAO by a principal, teacher or a parent, EQAO initially contacts the school and/or the school board for more information. Depending on the outcome of this preliminary step, EQAO may require the school/board to conduct an investigation and provide the agency with a report of its findings. Concurrently, the agency conducts a database check on the school data and/or pulls student booklets for review depending on the circumstances. Ultimately, EQAO decides whether or not to release individual student, school or board results. The decision rests on whether the agency is confident in the integrity of the results. It is the responsibility of the school board to take any disciplinary action it deems necessary regarding personnel issues that are internal to the board.

APPEALS

Due to the relatively low-stakes nature of EQAO's Primary, Junior and Grade 9 assessments, appeals of student results are not entertained. For the high-stakes OSSLT, however, appeals are received but only under specific conditions. Appeals based on questions of scoring accuracy are not accepted. EQAO has implemented rigorous scoring procedures (further details are provided in Chapter 6) for the OSSLT which includes double scoring of students' open responses. In cases where two scores for a given item vary by more than one score point/code, the item is scored for a third time by an expert scorer (adjudication scoring). Consequently, a total of at least 16 different scorers provide scores for each student's eight open-response items. Given this approach to scoring, a student is only eligible for an appeal when he/she claims to have written responses to questions/tasks, but one or more of these responses are reported as missing or blank on various EQAO data reports. In such cases, the appeal must be launched by the school principal on behalf of the student.

SUMMARY

This chapter highlights two main topics: the importance of providing relevant information about expected test-administration procedures to those who need it and the requirement of quality assurance in test administration. Test developers or testing organizations/agencies need to provide test takers and others either directly or indirectly affected by the assessment with an appropriate amount of information about the content and form of the assessment. Teachers, students and their parents/guardians need to know what the test will look like, how the students' work will be scored and what good work looks like. Information about test administration, accommodations, deferrals, exemptions and the appeals process of student results (where appropriate) also need to be made public. Quality assurance procedures must be instituted so that those receiving the test results, including the public and the testing organization itself, have confidence that the test was administered fairly and consistently across the jurisdiction, and that the test results are reliable and can be validly interpreted. The future of any large-scale assessment program rests largely on its integrity and the confidence it instills.

CHAPTER SIX

OPEN-RESPONSE SCORING

ETHICAL CONSIDERATIONS

Ethical principles dictate that there needs to be consistent and fair procedures to guide the process of judging the quality of a performance or product, or the degree of correctness of an answer. Scoring of students' open responses usually involves human beings who bring an element of subjectivity to the scoring activity. If they are teachers, they may bring a mindset oriented to classroom marking that reflects different purposes, approaches and methods of reporting than is the case with large-scale assessment. Consequently, there is a need in large-scale assessment to provide scorers with rigorous training in the use of scoring rubrics that contain the requirements for the codes/scores that describe the various degrees of success on an open-response test item. In addition, scoring guides provide examples of student work for each score code on the rubric.

Other aspects of ethics in open-response scoring relate to the background and experience of scorers and the procedures used to ensure scoring validity and reliability. In terms of scorer background and experience, certain professional standards should apply. For example, if the student work to be scored is high-school mathematics, it may be necessary to engage teachers of high-school mathematics or non-teachers with university/college degrees in mathematics. Some large-scale assessment programs insist that educators score student work; in other instances, professional scorers are used who may or may not be educators. In terms of scoring validity and inter-rater reliability, scorers need to be trained to accurately (validly) and consistently (reliably) apply the scoring rubrics and guides, and procedures should be in place to constantly monitor the validity and reliability of scoring over the scoring session and from one year to the next. In any case, the goal of the training is to ensure that all scorers would give the same student response the same score.

APPROACHES TO SCORING

Worldwide, many large-scale assessment programs score students' open-response work in a paper-based environment. This means that student booklets/responses are physically distributed to scorers (in some jurisdictions scorers are referred to as readers or markers), usually in central or regional scoring locations. In recent years, however, numerous jurisdictions have moved to image-based scoring, which may involve capturing student work while the assessment is in progress or scanning student work from paper booklets following an assessment.

The advantage of image-based scoring is that the complex routing of test booklets is reduced; images of student work are routed electronically to scorers. Most image-based scoring systems also have online training, monitoring of scoring validity and reliability and retraining/moderation components built into them. These functions can result in increased efficiencies compared to paper-based scoring. In addition, image-based scoring provides opportunities for distributed scoring in which the students' open responses can be distributed online to scorers at home. This can result in efficiencies if scorers are able to score at any time, rather than at the fixed times of a scoring site. Furthermore, with the paper-based, centralized/regional approach, some highly qualified scorers are unable to participate because of transportation issues or because they are unable to leave their classrooms for extended periods of time. Image-based, distributed scoring overcomes this barrier.

If a jurisdiction wishes to design its own scoring system and put it into operation, the initial financial and continuing maintenance costs, as well as the time required to research and implement an image-based scoring system may be prohibitive. Consequently, most jurisdictions acquire image-based scoring services/systems through contractors/vendors.

More recently, significant progress has been made in the computerized scoring of open-response items using artificial intelligence. If this approach results in accurate and consistent scoring, it may provide important efficiencies for assessment programs in the future.

There are two major types of scoring: analytic and holistic. Analytic scoring involves identifying aspects of the open response and then scoring each aspect using four to six levels representing different levels of proficiency. For example, aspects of a written response might include the quality of ideas about an issue in the argument presented; the ability to organize, develop, and express those ideas; relevant supporting reasons and examples used; and the ability to control the elements of standard written English. Holistic scoring involves rating the overall proficiency level of a student's writing using a well-developed scoring rubric with generally four proficiency levels. When holistic scoring is used, scorers do not attend to any one aspect of the writing but consider the response as a whole. Further, an holistic score is not the total or average of the aspect scores obtained in analytic scoring; rather, it is a reflection of the overall written response. Holistic scoring is generally faster than analytic scoring but does not provide feedback in the way that analytic scoring does. The question of speed of scoring is crucial in the case of large-scale assessments and the need to provide the results to schools, teachers and students in a short period of time following the administration of the assessment. But if there are sufficient resources, analytic scoring would be preferred if the purpose of the assessment is to provide more specific feedback to students. Having said this, most large-scale testing organizations use holistic scoring given the large number of students assessed and the need to report results quickly.

EQAO SCORING PROCESS

The present EQAO scoring process uses holistic scoring and is paper-based. As is the case in most large-scale assessments, the students' multiple-choice responses are machine-scored except for the Primary (Grade 3) assessments, which are entered manually into the computer with 100% verification. The scoring of the open-response items is conducted centrally in Toronto and uses the paper-based approach. The open-response items for the Primary, Junior and Grade 9 assessments are holistically scored by qualified Ontario educators. It is relatively easy to attract practicing teachers and principals, since the scoring is conducted during the first two weeks of July during summer vacation.

Since successful completion of the OSSLT is a graduation requirement and many of the students are in their last year of school, the results for all students must be reported in early June (the end of the school year) to allow principals and teachers of the students in the 12th Grade to determine if the students have qualified for the required literacy credit. Consequently, the test is administered in late March/early April, and the responses to the open-response items are holistically scored during approximately two weeks immediately following test administration. Since scoring occurs during the school year, it is difficult for teachers to be released from their classes for any significant amount of time to score. Consequently, EQAO seconds a relatively small number of practicing teachers but limits the amount of time they will be out of the classroom, recruits as many members of the Ontario College of Teachers as possible who are not teaching (many of them retired teachers) and engages a number of individuals with university degrees, so that the number of scorers is sufficient to score open-response items during the two-week scoring period. The individuals with university degrees are initially screened, including taking a written language test to ensure they have sufficient proficiency in either the English or French Language to read and validly and reliably score the students' responses to the open-response items. While the majority of the scorers for the open-response items requiring a short response are individuals with university degrees, some of the scorers for these items are practicing and retired teachers. The opposite is true for the two open-response items requiring an extended response; the majority of scorers are members of the Ontario College of Teachers (practicing or retired teachers) and some are individuals with other university degrees.

EQAO's scoring process involves four main steps – range finding, preparation of scoring materials, operational scoring and field-test scoring. Each of these steps, with sub-steps where they occur, is described below.

Pre-Range Finding and Range Finding

Range finding (called anchor selection in some jurisdictions) is a foundational process in scoring. Its purpose is to ensure that high-quality training and scoring materials are prepared for the scoring session, so that accurate and consistent scoring of student work is accomplished. It is through range finding that examples of student work are identified and used to train the scorers. Before range finding can occur, however, pre-range finding must take place.

Pre-range Finding

Pre-range finding is completed by EQAO education officers. Upon receipt of student test materials from schools, they first select a purposeful sample (considering factors such as geographic region, gender, English-language learners, students with special needs) of approximately 500 student responses for each open-response item. (The numbers of French-Language student responses available for pre-range finding are fewer due to the relatively small student population.) The criteria used to select these items include evidence that students were able to respond appropriately to the items and that the open-response items elicited an appropriate range of responses that can be scored on the rubric. Responses that are difficult to read (e.g., student handwriting that is not clear; responses that do not lend themselves to quality photocopies) are not selected. From this point, pre-range-finding activities only continue for open-response items that appear to have worked well with students.

The education officers review and then sort the booklets for the retained items into four piles based on the quality of responses: low, medium, high and mixed. For operational test items, approximately 30 booklets are chosen for each of the low, medium and high piles, and about 40 are chosen for the mixed pile. They represent the full range of student responses within piles and across the full range of responses. For example, within the low category, the responses should reflect the range from the weakest to the strongest performance within the low category. In addition, the range of responses includes those that are off-topic (this does not apply to mathematics), incorrect, typical or unusual; blanks are not selected. For matrix items, booklets are sorted by codes 10, 20, 30 and 40.

Range Finding

Following the pre-range-finding activity, EQAO involves eight to ten practicing principals and teachers for each assessment to conduct range finding. Range-Finding Committee members for each assessment have the following qualifications:

- Expertise and experience in the application of scoring rubrics based on the Achievement Charts in *The Ontario Curriculum*
- The ability to explain clearly and concisely the reasons why a student response is at one of the codes in a rubric

- Expertise in and current experience with the curriculum and the students in the grade for the assessment

Under the supervision of the agency's education officers, these committee members review the materials sorted during pre-range finding and discuss each item or prompt together with its scoring rubric. They then

- select representative samples of student responses to illustrate the performances that reflect the range of student responses at each of the codes of the scoring rubrics;
- make recommendations for refinements to the item-specific rubrics and to the wording of the annotations that explain the assigned codes;
- provide expert coding of student responses that will be used to train scorers;
- provide expert coding of student responses that will be used to assess scoring accuracy;
- select anchor papers that demonstrate the "true" score/code for each item;
- select papers to be used for calibration during scoring;
- discuss the procedures and potential scoring issues for scorer training and
- provide expert coding of the student responses that will be used in the qualifying test that the scorers must pass before becoming a scorer and for a parallel test that scorers who failed the first time take after some additional training.

Preparation of Final Scoring Materials

EQAO's education officers, under the supervision of their respective program managers, are responsible for ensuring that the following materials (the first four of which will be used to train and accredit scorers and the last two that will be used during operational scoring) are available:

- Scoring rubrics (item-specific and/or generic)
- Anchor papers (student responses that solidly represent each of the

score points/codes in the scoring rubrics including annotations that explain why they have been selected)

- Training papers (student responses that both solidly represent each of the score points/codes including annotations for scoring leaders' and supervisors' use)

- Qualifying tests (that contain responses with solid scores/codes)

- Calibration papers used during operational item scoring for ongoing training purposes (student responses that are more challenging to score such as those that are unusual, are relatively short and contain a blend of strong and weak attributes)

- Validity papers (student responses that solidly represent each of the score points/codes in the scoring rubrics and are used during operational item scoring to monitor scoring accuracy)

Operational Scoring

Personnel and Timing

Operational scoring of the Primary, Junior and Grade 9 assessments takes place during the first half of July. The Primary and Junior operational scoring session is a two-week process; the Grade 9 assessment is scored during a single week. A total of approximately 1,230 educators (English) and 210 (French) are required to score the Primary and Junior assessments; a total of approximately 275 educators (English) and 25 (French) are required to score the Grade 9 assessment. A scoring leader is responsible for each scoring room, and each room is divided into "pods" (groupings), each overseen by a scoring supervisor. The ratio of scoring supervisors to scorers is approximately 1/20 to 1/25 for each assessment.

Operational scoring of the OSSLT occurs over a two-week period in early April immediately following test administration. A total of approximately 1,550 scorers (English) and 125 (French) are required to score the students' work. The ratio of scoring leaders and supervisors to scorers is similar to that for the Primary, Junior and Grade 9 assessments. For all assessments, additional numbers of scorers (up to about 10%) are hired to account for those who decide not to participate (no-shows) and for attrition.

Management of the scoring site also requires significant involvement of EQAO staff. Approximately 25 members of the Assessment and Reporting unit and up to 40 staff members from other units such as Communications, Data Management and Analysis, Finance, Human Resources, Information Technology, Operations and Psychometrics and are on hand to oversee various aspects of receiving and scoring.

A limited number of assessment items (usually one or two items in language and four in mathematics) is scored in each scoring room under the supervision of a scoring leader (who is responsible for the whole room) and scoring supervisors (who are responsible for a pod of 20 to 25 scorers in the room). The scoring leaders, in collaboration with the supervisors, provide the training; monitor the scoring validity, reliability and productivity and re-train scorers as required.

Scoring Leader and Supervisor Training

Scoring leaders must have subject expertise, experience as scorers (and usually as scoring supervisors of EQAO assessments) and possess skills in adult learning in order to work effectively with scorers. Scoring supervisors are selected from a pool of experienced and effective EQAO scorers.

The training of the scoring leaders and supervisors is conducted just prior to the scoring session. EQAO's education officers train the scoring leaders who in turn train the scoring supervisors under the supervision of the education officers. The training of scoring leaders and supervisors contains the same elements as scorer training (see next subsection) and includes an explanation of the operation of the scoring centre, ways to monitor the scoring in their room and their responsibilities in monitoring scoring accuracy, consistency and productivity, which are explained in detail later in this chapter.

Following their training and just prior to the commencement of scoring, the scoring leaders and supervisors must take the qualifying test for their scoring room and attain at least 80% exact and 100% exact plus adjacent agreement with codes expertly assigned to samples of student responses in order to be certified.

Scorer Training

One of the most challenging roles of the scoring leader is to encourage scorers to let go of any preconceived ideas about scoring they may have from their classroom marking experience, and they must train the scorers to apply the scoring materials and procedures consistently and accurately. Scoring should not involve a lot of subjective judgement, but rather it should be a matching exercise in which scorers match student responses to the anchors and rubric descriptors. The objective of training is to ensure that all scorers become experts in scoring the small number of items for which they are responsible.

Scorer training takes approximately one-half day to complete and includes the following components:

- An overview of the assessment
- Instructions about test security and confidentiality
- Instructions on how to enter codes into the personal digital assistants (PDA's) that are used to gather the scored data
- A thorough training and discussion of scoring materials (including anchors and rubrics) and how individual items are to be coded
- Scoring and discussing a practice set of training papers to internalize the rubrics

Once the training has been conducted, each scorer must pass the qualifying test for the scoring room before he/she can score student work. The scorers must demonstrate their understanding of and ability to apply the rubrics by attaining at least 70% exact agreement with codes assigned to sample student work during range finding. If they do not meet the exact agreement standard, the scorers are retrained and retested. If they continue to be unable to meet the standard they are dismissed.

Scoring Procedures

Since the Primary, Junior and Grade 9 assessments are considered relatively low stakes, the open responses are scored once. To monitor scoring validity (accuracy), each scorer scores sets of validity papers (expertly scored student responses) each day, and scoring accuracy is assessed by examining the agreement between the scores assigned by the scorer and those assigned by the experts prior to scoring. Inter-rater reliability (scoring consistency) is assessed by examining the agreement between the scores assigned by the scorers to the other open-response items in the booklets containing the validity papers. Since the OSSLT is a high-stakes assessment, each open-response item included in the OSSLT is scored independently by two scorers. If the two scores/codes are non-adjacent (meaning the code assigned by one scorer is more than one code below or above that of the other scorer), the response is scored for a third time by an expert scorer (a consistently valid scorer, education officer or scoring leader) to determine the correct score for the student. Scoring consistency (inter-rater reliability) for the OSSLT is assessed by examining the agreement between the scores assigned by the two independent scorers. More detail about monitoring of scoring is provided under the heading "Scoring Centre Reports."

Scoring Centre Reports

Each day, the scoring leaders and supervisors are provided with scoring centre reports that show a variety of data related to scoring accuracy, consistency and productivity.

During scoring, EQAO monitors scoring accuracy through the use of validity booklets and validity statistics. Validity booklets contain at least one open-response item that was expertly scored during range finding and validated by education officers prior to scoring. During scoring, each scorer scores at least one but ideally up to ten validity booklets per day. By comparing the scorers' scores with those assigned by the experts (considered the "true" scores) the accuracy of scoring can be judged. The validity criteria, which are in line with industry standards, are as follows:

- For three-point rubrics:
  75% exact and 95% exact plus adjacent agreement
- For four-point rubrics:
  70% exact and 95% exact plus adjacent agreement
- For five-point rubrics:
  65% exact and 95% exact plus adjacent agreement
- For six-point rubrics:
  60% exact and 95% exact plus adjacent agreement

Scoring leaders and supervisors use the validity data to monitor individual and group scoring accuracy. If, after scoring at least 10 validity booklets, a scorer is below the required standard, re-training occurs. If re-training does not correct the situation, then the scorer may be dismissed. The scores of dismissed scorers are audited and re-scored if necessary. If group validity is below the required standard, re-training of the group will occur.

To illustrate how EQAO uses the scoring validity data, consider the abbreviated Daily Scorer Intervention Validity Report for Grade 9 Mathematics open-response items 8, 9, 10 and 11 provided in Table 16.

As shown in Table 16, there are 23 scorers (the actual number of scorers for these four items was approximately 70). The daily validity coefficients that fail to meet the exact agreement and that fail to meet the exact plus adjacent criteria are highlighted. For example, for question 8, eight scorers (scorers 1 to 8) have unacceptable exact validity; of these scorers, all but one (scorer 5) have acceptable exact plus adjacent validity. An examination of whether a scorer is assigning relatively high (high adjacent, high non-adjacent) codes or relatively low (low adjacent, low non-adjacent) codes provides scoring leaders and supervisors with valuable information with which to work with scorers on their scoring accuracy. (It should be pointed out that in the case of Table 16, all of the scorers have relatively small numbers of validity reads. A good rule of thumb is that at least 10 validity reads are required for a scorer before judgements about his/her scoring accuracy can be made with confidence. Although their validity metrics must be interpreted with some caution, the performance of these scorers would be monitored as the number of reads increases, and re-training would be conducted as required.) Several other types of scoring centre reports, including cumulative validity and inter-rater reliability, are also generated daily and as needed.

Scorer consistency is determined by looking at the agreement between two scorers who independently scored the same response. As mentioned previously, Primary, Junior and Grade 9 assessment open responses are single-scored. However, all scorers in a scoring room score the same validity booklets. Inter-rater reliability (scoring consistency) is assessed by examining the amount of agreement between score codes assigned by two independent scorers for items in the validity booklets that are not used for the validity process. All OSSLT open responses are independently scored by two scorers. In this case, the inter-rater reliability is assessed by examining the amount of agreement between score codes assigned by two independent scorers. The criteria for inter-rater reliability are the same as those for the validity papers.

Senior management at the scoring site uses the inter-rater reliability data to monitor group scoring consistency. If inter-rater reliability is below the required standard at the pod/group or room level, the possible reason(s) for the lack of consistency are examined, and corrective action is taken as appropriate.

Daily and cumulative mean score and score-point distribution data are used to monitor individual scorer and room scoring drift. After scoring a number of responses, scorers may unconsciously begin to assign higher or lower scores/codes. Therefore, to maintain consistency and accuracy in scoring, it is important to monitor for drift.

TABLE 16: Daily Scorer Intervention Validity Report — Grade 9 Assessment of Mathematics, Questions 8, 9, 10 and 11

Scorer ID	Q8							Q9						
	Validity Reads	Exact plus Adjacent %	Low Non-Adjacent %	Low Adjacent %	Exact %	High Adjacent %	High Non-Adjacent %	Validity Reads	Exact plus Adjacent %	Low Non-Adjacent %	Low Adjacent %	Exact %	High Adjacent %	High Non-Adjacent %
1	1	100	0	100	0	0	0	1	100	0	100	0	0	0
2	3	100	0	0	67	33	0	0						
3	2	100	0	50	50	0	0	3	100	0	0	67	33	0
4	2	100	0	0	50	50	0	2	100	0	0	100	0	0
5	1	0	0	0	0	0	100	3	100	0	0	100	0	0
6	3	100	0	0	67	33	0	2	100	0	0	100	0	0
7	2	100	0	50	50	0	0	4	100	0	0	100	0	0
8	2	100	0	50	50	0	0	6	100	0	0	100	0	0
9	3	100	0	0	100	0	0	1	100	0	0	100	0	0
10	4	100	0	0	100	0	0	2	100	0	0	50	50	0
11	3	100	0	0	100	0	0	3	100	0	0	67	33	0
12	1	100	0	0	100	0	0	1	100	0	100	0	0	0
13	3	100	0	0	100	0	0	2	100	0	0	50	50	0
14	0							3	100	0	0	67	33	0
15	3	100	0	0	100	0	0	2	100	0	0	50	50	0
16	2	100	0	0	100	0	0	3	100	0	0	100	0	0
17	4	100	0	0	100	0	0	3	100	0	0	100	0	0
18	2	100	0	0	100	0	0	1	100	0	0	100	0	0
19	3	100	0	0	100	0	0	2	100	0	0	100	0	0
20	4	100	0	0	100	0	0	1	100	0	0	100	0	0
21	0							1	100	0	0	100	0	0
22	4	100	0	0	100	0	0	1	100	0	0	100	0	0
23	3	100	0	0	100	0	0	1	100	0	0	100	0	0
Average	2.3	99.3			88.3			2.3	100			87		

Acceptable metrics (Exact): 70% (Exact plus Adjacent): 95% Scoring Room:

	Q10							Q11					
Validity Reads	Exact plus Adjacent %	Low Non-Adjacent %	Low Adjacent %	Exact %	High Adjacent %	High Non-Adjacent %	Validity Reads	Exact plus Adjacent %	Low Non-Adjacent %	Low Adjacent %	Exact %	High Adjacent %	High Non-Adjacent %
1	100	0	100	0	0	0	4	100	0	75	25	0	0
1	100	0	100	0	0	0	2	100	0	0	100	0	0
3	100	0	0	100	0	0	2	100	0	0	100	0	0
2	100	0	0	100	0	0	3	100	0	0	67	33	0
3	100	0	0	100	0	0	2	100	0	0	100	100	0
1	100	0	0	100	0	0	0						
3	100	0	33	67	0	0	3	67	33	0	33	33	0
0							3	100	0	33	33	33	0
1	100	0	0	100	0	0	5	100	0	40	40	20	0
3	100	0	67	33	0	0	1	0	100	0	0	0	0
4	100	0	25	75	0	0	1	100	0	0	100	0	0
4	100	0	0	100	0	0	3	100	0	0	67	33	0
2	100	0	0	100	0	0	1	100	0	0	100	0	0
2	100	0	0	100	0	0	6	100	0	33	50	17	0
1	100	0	0	100	0	0	4	100	0	25	50	25	0
7	100	0	14	86	0	0	3	100	0	33	67	0	0
3	100	0	33	67	0	0	1	100	0	0	100	0	0
4	100	0	0	100	0	0	3	100	0	0	33	67	0
3	100	0	0	100	0	0	2	100	0	0	0	100	0
2	100	0	50	50	0	0	1	100	0	0	100	0	0
4	100	0	50	50	0	0	6	100	0	17	67	17	0
6	100	0	33	67	0	0	1	100	0	0	0	100	0
1	100	0	0	100	0	0	3	100	0	33	67	0	0
2.8	99.4			84.3			2.4	97.9			68.5		

Source: Adapted from EQAO records; © by EQAO, used with permission.

TABLE 17: Mean Score and Score Point Distribution Report — Grade 9 Assessment of Mathematics, Questions 8, 9, 10 and 11

	Percent at Each Score Point													
	Q8								Q9						
Scorer ID	Total Reads	Mean Score	B	I	Code 10	Code 20	Code 30	Code 40	Total Reads	Mean Score	B	I	Code 10	Code 20	Code 30	Code 40
1	333	2.3	11	1	21	20	20	28	333	2.2	6	1	23	15	46	8
2	358	2.4	19	2	14	10	17	38	358	2.2	16	1	7	26	41	8
3	322	2.4	15	2	14	13	22	34	322	2.2	14	2	8	26	43	8
4	312	2.4	7	1	22	16	23	30	312	2.4	6	1	9	33	41	9
5	396	2.4	11	4	18	13	20	35	396	2.4	6	1	8	32	40	12
6	398	2.5	10	3	19	12	18	38	398	2.3	7	2	17	19	46	9
7	507	2.5	9	1	21	15	19	36	507	2.3	6	2	18	21	44	9
8	369	2.5	7	6	15	13	23	36	369	2.5	8	2	5	18	54	12
9	365	2.6	6	3	17	14	22	38	365	2.2	6	4	13	29	41	8
10	277	2.6	16	0	10	8	27	38	277	2.3	17	2	5	12	56	8
11	354	2.6	14	2	10	10	29	35	354	2.3	13	1	12	17	47	11
12	342	2.6	10	0	14	16	20	40	342	2.3	8	0	11	32	40	9
13	384	2.6	8	1	16	15	20	40	384	2.4	5	1	9	31	44	9
14	563	2.6	10	2	13	13	23	38	563	2.4	7	2	6	33	42	11
15	276	2.6	10	1	16	14	19	39	276	2.4	4	1	8	30	49	7
16	393	2.6	5	4	13	16	27	35	393	2.4	2	3	19	16	47	13
17	372	2.6	9	4	7	18	26	35	372	2.5	5	1	11	25	47	11
18	327	2.6	9	2	15	14	25	35	327	2.6	7	2	6	11	66	9
19	430	2.7	6	3	16	12	24	39	430	2.3	6	2	12	26	47	6
20	282	2.8	9	1	11	12	27	40	282	2.4	4	2	12	28	45	8
21	364	2.8	6	3	10	14	27	40	364	2.4	6	2	10	26	44	12
22	311	2.8	6	2	10	17	25	40	311	2.4	5	1	13	21	52	8
23	313	2.9	7	0	6	19	21	47	313	2.5	5	1	6	30	46	12
Average	363	2.6	10	2.1	14	14	23	37	363	2.4	7	1.6	11	24	46	10

LARGE-SCALE ASSESSMENT ISSUES AND PRACTICES: AN INTRODUCTORY HANDBOOK

Scoring Room:

| Percent at Each Score Point ||||||||||||||
| Q10 |||||||| Q11 ||||||
Total Reads	Mean Score	B	I	Code 10	Code 20	Code 30	Code 40	Total Reads	Mean Score	B	I	Code 10	Code 20	Code 30	Code 40
333	1.8	22	1	26	21	12	18	333	1.7	22	1	35	15	4	23
358	1.5	29	3	27	18	9	15	358	1.6	29	2	27	14	4	23
322	1.6	29	2	26	15	14	15	322	1.5	26	3	34	16	2	20
312	1.7	17	1	30	25	17	11	312	1.6	20	2	38	14	9	17
396	1.7	23	3	24	19	14	16	396	1.7	20	2	39	14	3	24
398	1.5	25	3	28	19	14	11	398	1.7	21	4	35	12	5	23
507	1.7	21	6	21	22	11	19	507	1.5	23	4	35	15	1	21
369	1.6	23	3	24	25	11	15	369	1.6	23	2	39	9	2	25
365	1.6	21	3	30	20	14	12	365	1.8	16	3	36	18	6	22
277	1.4	29	2	23	24	16	7	277	1.7	26	1	29	14	5	25
354	1.6	27	1	23	24	13	12	354	1.7	23	1	34	16	3	23
342	1.7	22	1	27	20	14	15	342	1.6	25	1	36	13	2	22
384	1.5	23	3	31	19	13	12	384	1.5	25	2	35	15	3	19
563	1.6	24	3	29	16	10	17	563	1.6	23	1	38	11	5	22
276	1.7	18	2	29	24	14	13	276	1.6	22	3	39	11	5	20
393	1.8	21	4	27	13	17	18	393	1.8	18	3	34	17	3	25
372	1.6	23	2	27	21	15	13	372	1.6	22	2	38	11	2	24
327	1.6	22	1	29	21	12	14	327	1.6	24	2	31	19	5	20
430	1.8	20	2	28	17	12	20	430	1.8	17	2	34	18	2	27
282	1.5	20	4	35	21	11	9	282	1.6	20	5	37	12	4	22
364	1.6	19	5	30	22	12	12	364	1.8	18	5	35	9	5	28
311	1.7	19	4	26	22	14	15	311	1.7	21	2	36	15	5	21
313	1.9	20	2	26	16	14	22	313	1.7	22	2	34	15	1	27
363	1.6	23	2.7	27	20	13	14.7	363	1.7	22	2.4	35	14	4	23

Source: Adapted from EQAO records; © by EQAO, used with permission.

Daily and cumulative mean score and score point distribution data are also useful in pinpointing problems that scorers with low validity are having. EQAO uses these data to inform individual and group-level intervention. The distribution of percentages at each score point/code can help scoring leaders and supervisors determine whether a given scorer or group of scorers is assigning codes relatively higher or lower than the room average. Armed with this information (together with validity statistics), the scoring leaders and supervisors are well equipped to intervene with/retrain scorers. Whenever scoring drift is identified, it is best practice to re-reference scorers to the training materials and, in particular, the anchor papers. Daily review of anchors, rubrics and calibration papers serves to mitigate scoring drift. Table 17 is a sample scoring centre report that provides individual scorer data on mean scores and score-point distributions.

For an item that is scored using four codes one would expect the mean score to be in the area of approximately 2.2 to 2.8. The mean scores on items 8 and 9 are in this range. (The room average appears on the bottom row of the table.) However, the mean scores of items 10 and 11 are below 2.0. It may well be that these two items are particularly challenging, but it is unusual to see the relatively large percentages of student responses for these two items given a code 10. In addition, the percentage of blanks (B) identified for these two items is relatively large. An examination of the items and potentially how the scoring rubrics are being applied would be in order.

The scoring of open-response items needs to be completed in a fixed time period determined by the time at which the results of the assessment are to be reported to school boards, schools, and students. Usually this period is one to three weeks, depending on the complexity of the scoring and the budget allocated to it. Once the scoring begins, productivity needs to be monitored on a daily basis to ensure that all the scoring is completed in the time allotted for scoring and on budget. For example, EQAO monitors the productivity of each scoring room through daily productivity reports. The number of papers scored the previous day and up to the previous day, the expected number of days remaining to complete the scoring, the productivity target for the day and the minimum acceptable number of papers to be scored for the day are provided daily to each scoring room. The reports also contain daily and cumulative productivity data for each scorer, each pod/group and for the room as a whole. The scoring leaders and supervisors review and use the productivity data to determine whether individual scorers, the pod/group or the room as a whole needs to increase productivity, and, if so, what interventions are needed. These data are also used to monitor the progress across the scoring rooms to plan any scorer movements among groups/rooms that may be necessary to ensure all of the scoring rooms finish on time.

Table 18 contains a sample productivity summary report by scoring room for the Grade 9 Academic and Applied Mathematics assessments administered in January (Winter) and June (Spring).

This report was produced at the end of day two of a five-day scoring session. The report shows that based on the current number of scorers in the rooms and productivity through Day 2, three English-language and five French-language scoring rooms (highlighted) may not finish on time. In these cases, productivity needs to be increased, and at a certain point during the next three days the decision might be made to transfer a given number of scorers from rooms that will finish early to rooms that are behind. The objective is to have all scorers complete their work at the end of day five, which is a delicate balancing act that requires constant monitoring of productivity.

Other Procedures (Exceptions, Students at Risk, Audits)

Booklets that contain offensive language, are damaged or misprinted or contain possible evidence of irregularities in test administration are sent to an Exceptions Room for review by a quality assurance panel consisting of an education officer, the Program Manager, Director of Assessment and Reporting and Chief Assessment Officer. If the booklets contain obscene, racist or sexist content, the material is shared with the school principal for follow-up with the student.

Sometimes, booklets are torn, misstapled, have missing pages or have barcodes that have been damaged and therefore cannot be scanned. In such cases, students are not be penalized. Exceptions Room and Data Management and Analysis staff attempt to find missing information, and if necessary, calls are made to schools in an attempt to find missing student work. In some cases, the quality assurance panel may determine that the student's scores should be pro-rated based on the results of available responses.

The existence of different types of handwriting and similar patterns of student responses may indicate the possibility of some form of irregularity in test administration. These situations require a great deal of care because often different handwriting may be explained by the students having scribes recording answers for them. Likewise, similar patterns in student responses may be explained by the instructional methods used by the teacher and may not be indicative of an irregularity. The quality assurance panel discusses these situations and in some cases follows up with school principals or school board personnel for further information and possible investigation.

Occasionally, a student's response to an open-response item contains evidence that he/she may be at risk for abuse or neglect, or the content of a response may explicitly or implicitly suggest threats of violence to him/herself or to others. In such cases, the scorer who raises the concern has the legal duty and responsibility to report it to the local Childrens' Aid Society (CAS). EQAO has established a process to assist the scorer to inform the CAS.

Field-Test Scoring

The embedded open-response field-test items are scored either during the scoring of the operational open-response items or immediately after operational scoring is completed. These field-test items are scored by the most accurate, reliable and productive scoring leaders, supervisors and scorers of the similar operational items. They are trained on these

TABLE 18: Overall Productivity Summary — Grade 9 Mathematics Scoring

Room	Current Information				Options		
	Current Left to Score	Current Average Productivity	Current Number of Scorers	Target Days to Finish	Number of Scorers Required (+/−)	Number of Days Required (+/−)	Rate Adjustment Required (+/−)
English Applied, January, Book 1 Questions 8, 9, 10, 11	13 430	311.8	18	3	14.4	2.4	248.7
English Applied, January, Book 2 Questions 26, 28, 29	14 126	338.6	16	3	13.9	2.6	294.3
English Academic, January, Book 1 Questions 8, 9, 10, 11	30 520	249.9	43	3	40.7	2.8	236.6
English Academic, January, Book 2 Questions 26, 28, 29	33 792	221.8	37	3	50.8	4.1	304.4
English Applied, June, Book 1 Questions 8, 9, 10, 11	19 062	261.5	23	3	24.3	3.2	276.3
English Applied, June, Book 2 Questions 26, 28, 29	17 797	360.9	19	3	16.4	2.6	312.2
English Academic, June, Book 1 Questions 8, 9, 10, 11	46 611	177.5	53	3	87.5	5.0	293.2
English Academic, June, Book 2 Questions 26, 28, 29	37 899	329.7	50	3	38.3	2.3	252.7
French Applied, January, Book 1 Questions 8, 9, 10, 11	671	48.0	2	3	4.7	7.0	111.8
French Applied, January, Book 2 Questions 26, 28, 29	511	103.5	2	3	1.6	2.5	85.2
French Academic, January, Book 1 Questions 8, 9, 10, 11	1 458	51.4	5	3	9.5	5.7	97.2
French Academic, January, Book 2 Questions 26, 28, 29	1 323	98.8	4	3	4.6	3.3	110.3
French Applied, June, Book 1 Questions 8, 9, 10, 11	526	113.0	2	3	1.6	2.3	87.7
French Applied, June, Book 2 Questions 26, 28, 29	352	203.5	2	3	0.6	0.9	58.7
French Academic, June, Book 1 Questions 8, 9, 10, 11	2 023	66.0	6	3	10.2	5.1	112.4
French Academic, June, Book 2 Questions 26, 28, 29	2 298	40.0	4	3	19.2	14.4	191.5

Source: Adapted from EQAO records; © by EQAO, used with permission.

new items and are expected to maintain the same high standards that are applied during the scoring of operational items. This is important because the field-test items are intended for use on future assessments, and they are used to equate assessments from one year to the next.

SUMMARY

This chapter demonstrates the importance of implementing procedures to ensure accuracy, consistency and productivity in scoring students' open responses. Recruiting the right scoring leaders, supervisors and scorers; developing and implementing high-quality training materials and procedures and rigorously monitoring the scoring process is integral to achieving the goals of accurately, consistently and efficiently scoring students' responses to open-response items.

CHAPTER SEVEN

STANDARD SETTING

ETHICAL CONSIDERATIONS

Earlier chapters of this handbook have demonstrated that in many large-scale assessments, student results are reported as categories of performance related to a range of scores. The number of categories may be two such as successful/unsuccessful or three or more with labels such as "below basic," "basic," "proficient" or "advanced." Regardless of whether the given assessment is relatively low- or high-stakes, it is important that students' performances be properly and fairly classified and described. The *Principles for Fair Student Assessment Practices for Education in Canada* (1993) states that test developers should do the following:

> Examine the need for local passing or cut-off scores… (p. 17)
> Explain how passing or cut-off scores were set… (p. 17)
> Provide for periodic review and revision of…passing or cut-off scores, and inform users (p. 15)

Before launching into a discussion of standard setting, it is important to make a distinction between establishing performance levels and standard setting. Performance levels are descriptive labels that describe what students know and can do (e.g., below basic, basic, proficient, advanced) and are established prior to standard setting. An initial description of the performance levels can often be derived from the curriculum documents used to establish the test blueprint (see Chapter 3). The final descriptions are then developed by examining a sample of students' work in each performance level. In this handbook, standard setting involves determining the cut-scores that differentiate performance levels from each other.

Given the importance of accurate and consistent classifications of student performance, and since the setting of performance standards includes subjective elements, it is crucial that standard-setting activities be credible. Professional guidelines for setting standards are available and the procedures outlined in this chapter follow these guidelines.

COMMON STANDARD-SETTING METHODS

Hambleton and Pitoniak (2006) describe several standard-setting methods; summary descriptions of some of the more common approaches to standard setting are presented below. The first methods described (Angoff, Nedelsky, Analytical Judgment and Bookmark) are based on judgements about test items; other methods presented (Borderline Group, Contrasting Groups and Body of Work) are based on judgements about potential examinees.

Angoff Method

The Angoff Method involves panelists providing their estimates of the probability that the minimally competent/borderline examinee will answer an item correctly (multiple-choice items are scored in two categories: correct/incorrect or yes/no). The item estimates for each panelist are summed for all panelists to produce the estimated cut-score for that judge. The mean (or median) of the judges' estimated cut-scores is the estimated cut-score for the panel, and the standard deviation (or semi-interquartile range) is a measure of the lack of agreement.

Typically, the Angoff Method is modified by adding one or two more rounds. Usually, some information about panelists' ratings and the students' performance, including item difficulty, is presented following Round One. Round Two might also involve providing impact data (the consequences of applying the panelists' cut-scores), although presenting these data is more common after Round Two because of the concern that panelists will be unduly influenced by the impact results if the data are presented too early in the sequence. Following discussion, the panelists separately re-set their cut-scores. Round Three may involve providing panelists with impact data, followed by discussion and then revision, separately, of the Round Two cut-scores. The Angoff procedure and its modifications were first developed for dichotomously scored test items. However, it has been expanded to include polytomously scored items and to performance items. In the case of polytomously scored items, panelists most often separately estimate the mean performance of students in each of the performance levels. In the case of performance assessment, the attributes of performance are first identified and listed. The panelists then estimate the proportion of students in each performance level who could perform each of the attributes.

Nedelsky Method

The Nedelsky Method can only be used with multiple-choice items. In this approach, panelists are asked to estimate the number of alternatives (answer choices) the borderline examinee would be able to identify as incorrect for an item. The estimated probability of success for that item equals the reciprocal of the number of alternatives remaining. The probability estimates of each panelist are summed for all items under consideration to derive the panelist's estimated cut-score. Then these are averaged across all panelists to obtain the panel's final estimated cut-score. Like Angoff, more than one round is usually used.

Another limitation of the Nedelsky procedure is that the only possible item probabilities for a four-option multiple-choice item are 0.25, 0.33, 0.50 and 1.00. In contrast, the Angoff probabilities can vary from 0.0 to 1.0. Gross (1985) proposed a modification of the Nedelsky procedure that respected the initial test-taking behavior of students and increased the values of the estimated probabilities.

Analytical Judgment

The Analytical Judgment method involves panelists reviewing samples of students' performances either item by item or by sections of the test (Plake & Hambleton, 2001). This procedure requires the selection of a set of student booklets that have been previously scored (although the scores are not revealed to the panelists) and which represent performance across the total score scale. The method is termed "analytical" because the panelists consider individual items or sections of the test, rather than considering the test in its entirety (holistic).

In this procedure (should there be four performance categories), the panelists place students' responses from the complete set of student booklets into one of 12 achievement categories (four performance categories each divided into low, medium and high). The panelists' judgements can be translated into cut-scores by averaging the scores of student papers that were classified as "high" in one performance category and those that were classified as "low" in the next higher performance category. The cut-scores established for each sub-set of test items can then be summed to obtain cut-scores for the total test.

Bookmark Method

According to Lin (2006) the strengths of the Bookmark Method are that it

- accommodates constructed-response as well as selected-response items;
- can be used with multiple cut-scores and test forms and
- reduces the cognitive complexity for panelists.

The method requires that panelists review booklets that are specially constructed with items ordered according to their level of difficulty. Panelists are provided with rubrics and samples of student work for the open-response items. The panelist's task is to identify, for a given performance standard/category, up to which item in the item-ordered booklet the borderline examinee should be able to show what they know and what they can do. The panelist places a bookmark between the items such that all items below the bookmark the student can do, and all items above the bookmark the student is likely unable to do. Cut-scores of the panel are derived through the use of the ability metric using an Item Response Theory (IRT) scaling method. More information on IRT is presented in Chapter 8. Like the previous procedures, the Bookmark generally involves three rounds. Following Round Three, performance standards are revised by looking at what students can and cannot do.

Unlike the foregoing methods that focus primarily on the test items, the following methods' primary focus is on judgements about examinees.

Borderline Group Method

The Borderline Group Method involves first identifying a group of minimally competent/borderline examinees for each performance standard/category using teachers' ratings. Test scores for these examinees are gathered and their median test score is used as the cut-score for each performance standard/category.

Contrasting Groups Method

The Contrasting Groups Method involves requiring panelists to identify examinees who are clearly above a given performance standard and other examinees who are clearly below the given performance standard. For each of these two groups the distribution of test scores is contrasted to establish the performance standard. This method can be used for situations where there are multiple performance standards by having panelists sort examinees into multiple performance categories. Finding the point of overlap in the examinees' scores on adjacent performance categories can be used to calculate the cut-score(s). Another approach involves selecting cut-scores that result in the fewest "false positives" and "false negatives" (students incorrectly classified as meeting a standard, and students incorrectly classified as not meeting a standard, respectively). Finding panelists who are familiar with examinees and their performance is challenging for both the Borderline Group and Contrasting Groups methods.

Body of Work Method

Radwan and Rogers (2006) explain that the Body of Work Method uses a holistic approach that differentiates examinees according to their level of performance on both multiple-choice and open-response test items. In general terms, this standard-setting procedure involves panelists reviewing complete sets of examinee test responses, sorted from lowest to highest total scores. The constructed-response items are presented first, followed by the multiple-choice items. Displays of students' responses to multiple-choice and open-response test items are also provided. The panelists' task is to assign each body of student work into one of the performance categories.

Among the standard-setting procedures outlined above, the Modified Angoff and Bookmark Methods are the most commonly used in North American large-scale assessment programs, followed by the Body of Work Method. Space limitations preclude providing detailed information about how to apply each of the methods listed above; however, their procedures can be found in reference books such as those by Cizek (2001) and Cizek and Bunch (2007). A series of articles describing the more common standard-setting procedures can also be found in the *Alberta Journal of Educational Research* (2006) 52 (1). In addition, Berk's (1986) work provides a tri-level classification scheme to categorize standard-setting procedures and 10 criteria with which to evaluate them.

TYPICAL STANDARD-SETTING STEPS

The following information from Hambleton and Pitoniak (2006) describes nine typical steps in setting standards on criterion-referenced tests.

1 Choose a Standard-Setting Method

The choice of which standard-setting method to use will depend on

- the formats of the items included in the test;
- the time and resources required by the method and the time and resources available;
- the testing organization's experience with the various methods available and
- the availability of validity evidence for the various methods.

2 Select a Standard-Setting Panel

The composition of the standard-setting panel is a key decision in setting cut-scores. Standard-setting panels should involve panelists (sometimes referred to as judges) who will represent the different stakeholder groups that are impacted by the assessment. Some large-scale assessment programs rely heavily on educators as panelists, while in other programs a mix of educators and non-educators is used.

A good example of this comes from Saskatchewan in the mid 1990's where two different approaches to standard-setting panel composition were used. Saskatchewan's curriculum evaluation program was designed to monitor the effectiveness of new provincial curriculum. This involved determining the effectiveness of curriculum implementation and identifying strengths and weaknesses in both the curriculum and in student learning. Because the program was designed to support curriculum and instructional improvement, standards were set by panels of educators experienced in the particular grade levels, as well as the philosophy and content of the curriculum. Saskatchewan's provincial learning assessment program, on the other hand, was meant to address the purpose of public accountability. Consequently, a wide range of education stakeholder groups was represented on the standard-setting panel. These groups included practicing teachers and representatives of teachers' federations, chamber of commerce, post-secondary institutions, school trustees' organization, educational administrators and Ministry of Education officials (Jones & Hunter, 1996).

It is important that the large-scale assessment organization give serious consideration to the issue of panel composition and that the membership on the panel is well documented. Not only should consideration be given to the constituencies that panelists represent, but also to the diversity of the jurisdiction in terms of elements such as culture, region, gender, occupation and experience. Lastly, it is critical that the members of the standard-setting panel have knowledge and understanding of the curriculum to which the assessment is referenced and the students who are taught that curriculum.

Often the question arises about the number of panelists that is required for standard setting. Certainly, financial resources will be an important consideration, but it is necessary to have sufficient numbers to derive dependable results. For many situations 10 to 15 panelists are considered acceptable; in large-scale assessments in education at least 15 to 30 panelists are viewed as desirable. If resources permit, it may also be useful to consider running two or more standard-setting activities so that their results can be compared. If two or more panels set similar standards, this provides additional evidence for confidence in the performance standards (Hambleton & Pitoniak, 2006).

It is also important that the person(s) conducting the standard-setting session is experienced in the method to be used. This person will be responsible for the orientation and training of panelists, the materials to be used to train the panelists and to set the standard, and the process to be followed.

3 Develop Performance Category Descriptions

As indicated at the beginning of this chapter, it is necessary to have descriptions of performance categories (e.g., pass and fail; master and non-master; below basic, basic, proficient, advanced; Level 1, Level 2, Level 3, Level 4). The performance standards describe the performance of each category in terms of what examinees at that category know and can do. They provide qualitative descriptions of the knowledge, skills and behaviors individuals in each category possess. They must be stated in such a way that it is clear what the differences in knowledge, skills and behaviours between adjacent levels are. These statements can also be used to evaluate the relevance and representativeness of the items included in the assessment instruments and the procedures used to obtain the degree to which the examinees acquired the knowledge, skills and behaviours identified in the performance standards, so that valid interpretations about performance can be made (Rogers & Ricker, 2006, p. 18).

4 Provide Training to Panelists

Standard-setting panelists must be thoroughly trained to effectively apply the method to be used to determine the cut-score(s). They must be given opportunities to practice. Regardless of the approach used, training should include the following components:

- An orientation session including the purpose(s) of the test and the goals of the standard-setting process
- An explanation of the standard-setting procedures that will be followed
- An explanation and demonstration of test materials such as test content, multiple-choice item scoring keys and open-response item rubrics and anchors
- An appreciation of test-taking conditions (often panelists are given the opportunity to write the test or part of it as the examinees would have done; all of the procedures involve panelists taking multiple-choice items; in the case of short responses some methods require panelists to respond, while in other methods and with longer open-response items, examples [exemplars] of student work are provided)

- An explanation and demonstration of performance category descriptions
- Provision of a practice session and time to discuss the results of the practice session

5 Provide Judgements

Providing independent judgements about where the cut-scores should be in the score distribution is the key responsibility of the panelists. The manner in which the judgements are obtained depends on the standard-setting method selected, but usually the panelists enter their judgements on forms which are then taken and entered into a database by the individual or agency conducting the standard-setting session.

6 Provide Feedback and Facilitate Discussion

Typically, standard setting is conducted in two or three rounds. Summaries (mean, standard deviation) of panelists' cut-scores from Round 1 are shared with and discussed by the panel members so they hear what other panel members did as they set their cut-scores. Following this discussion, the panel members are invited to adjust their cut-scores in light of the discussion. Some standard-setting methods also involve sharing consequential data after the second round of judgments, meaning that if the panelists' cut-scores were used, what would the proportions of examinees be in each performance category? Following the sharing of consequential data, panelists are often given an opportunity to revise their cut-scores in a third round of judgements.

At each round, the variability among the panelists' cut-scores should be less than the variability in the previous round (i.e., a reduction in standard deviation or semi-interquartile range) after Round Two and again after Round Three. If, for example, the variability among panelists' cut-scores is small after the last round, then one can have confidence in the final cut-score(s). If variability is large, then one might have less confidence in the final cut-score(s).

7 Establish Cut-Score(s)

Once the cut-score process has been completed, the cut-scores of the individual panelists are compiled to determine the final cut-scores. The mean or median of the panelists' cut-scores are commonly used for this purpose. It is important to carefully document the entire process including panelists' cut-scores for the various rounds and the final recommendations.

8 Conduct Evaluation

At the end of the standard-setting process, panelists should complete an evaluation form that gathers information about their level of satisfaction with each of the steps in the process, any feedback or recommendations they might have to improve the process and their level of confidence and satisfaction with the cut-score(s) set. Documentation of this kind is critical information for supporting the validity of the performance standards and their accompanying cut-scores.

9 Compile Validity Evidence

It is extremely important to compile full documentation of all aspects of the standard-setting session, as soon as possible after the session has been completed, in order to have the fullest possible body of validity evidence for the process. This evidence consists of the documentation for setting the cut-scores and, after the assessment has been completed, the accuracy and consistency of the placement of the students in the performance categories. The term "accuracy" refers to the extent to which classifications based on observed student scores agree with the classifications based on the true scores of these students. The term "precision" refers to the extent to which classifications based on observed student scores on one form agree with the classifications of the observed scores of the same students on an interchangeable form. However, in large-scale assessments, the tests are administered only once to a student. In this case, procedures for estimating accuracy and consistency from the single test have been developed using classical test theory and item response theory. The selection of the approach to take should match the procedures used to analyze the items and equate the test forms from one year to the next. If procedures based on classical test theory are used to analyze the items and equate the tests, then the procedures used to determine accuracy and consistency should be based on classical test theory. If procedures based on item response theory are used to analyze the items and equate the tests, then the procedures used to determine accuracy and consistency should be based on item response theory.

CROSS-GRADE STANDARD SETTING

The foregoing discussion involves setting standards for categories of performance related to a range of scores on a single large-scale assessment. There is also a great deal of interest in developing performance standards that cross grades. This type of standard setting is referred to as vertically moderated standard setting (VMSS) or vertical articulation of standards.

Cizek (2005) identifies many of the challenges of establishing performance standards across grades. Among them is that criterion- or standards-based assessments are usually developed to specifications that are closely linked to grade-/subject-specific curriculum expectations/content standards that do not have a great deal of overlap. In addition, although curricula usually have a sequential aspect to them, most curricula are not developed as a continuous, developmental construct across grades.

Cizek describes VMSS, in its current state, as a process of smoothing cut-scores, in which a meta-panel of standard setters takes the "jagged" standards set by individual grade-level panels of standard setters (e.g., Grades 3, 4, 5, 6, 7, 8) and evens them out, so the peaks and valleys are eliminated and there is a smooth, continuous set of cut-scores across grades. In Cizek's opinion, VMSS is a fledgling concept and is in its early stages of development.

EQAO'S APPROACH TO STANDARD SETTING

Several standard-setting activities have been conducted since the initiation of the EQAO assessments. The following activities, related to the OSSLT administered to the English-language students, are presented here to demonstrate one approach used by the agency. A parallel set of activities was completed for the literacy test administered to the French-language students.

Prior to administering the first OSSLT in 2002, the agency conducted a standard-setting to establish the cut-scores for successful performance in both reading and writing, since at that time, these results were reported separately. Two full mornings were required to complete both components of the test, and students needed to be successful on both components to earn the OSSLT literacy credit.

In 2006, the OSSLT was re-designed to be administered in one morning and to adopt a single literacy score rather than two separate scores. Despite this change, the level of literacy required to be successful was to remain constant. It was necessary, therefore, that the cut-score required to be successful on the 2006 test be aligned with the level of performance needed to be successful prior to 2006 for both language groups.

The first step was to revise the description of successful performance on a single literacy test that included both reading and writing. Five literacy experts produced descriptions of the attributes that distinguished successful student performance from unsuccessful student performance on the 2006 OSSLT (Wilson, 2006). The experts used actual work of students who completed the 2004 OSSLT. They examined the reading performance and the writing performance and then developed a description of what a successful and unsuccessful student would do when the reading and writing tests became one test in 2006 and that required half of the 2004 administration time. The final qualitative descriptions captured what students should know and be able to do in reading and writing at the end of Grade 9.

Armed with the new performance descriptions for successful and unsuccessful students, a standard alignment activity was conducted (Plake, Rodeck & Davis, 2006). The following description of the standard alignment procedures is adapted from the final report of the study.

The standard alignment study was conducted in April, 2006 following the scoring of the 2006 OSSLT. There were two sets of panelists, one for French language comprised of 20 members and one for English language comprised of 16 members. In order to ensure that all panelists received the same messages, a bilingual orientation was provided to both language panels at the same time and that included information about the purpose of the standard alignment session and how the panels' work would inform policy making regarding the score to be successful on the OSSLT. Prior to their arrival at the session, the panelists had been advised to visit the EQAO Web site to review sample OSSLT test items.

Following the introductory orientation, the panelists were provided with an opportunity to experience the OSSLT in simulated test conditions in separate English- and French-language groups. First, they independently responded to multiple-choice and short-writing items and provided an outline of ideas for the long-writing item responses in the first test booklet. Next, they were given the second test booklet and the scoring keys for the two booklets, and they were asked to score their own work for Booklet 1 and then review Booklet 2.

Within each language group four smaller groups were created, two for reading and two for writing. The panelists then engaged in small-group discussions regarding the competencies required of the borderline (minimally competent) student to be successful on the OSSLT with reference to the table of specifications for the test and performance-level descriptors (the skills and achievements that differentiated students who had the skills to be successful on the OSSLT from those who did not) developed prior to the alignment activity (Wilson, 2006). The discussions were also informed by showing panelists samples of actual student work from the 2004 test for students whose scores were just at the cut point for reading and writing.

Following these orientation activities the panelists met in their separate language groups to experience a training/practice activity. The session involved panelists working through a set of eight OSSLT items, taken from previously administered tests that represented each of the item types: multiple-choice reading and writing, open-response reading and short- and long-writing prompts. The panelists practiced using the cut-score methods they would use in the standard alignment activity, and they also experienced the kinds of feedback they would receive during their deliberations.

Three different strategies were used by the panelists depending on the item type. For the multiple-choice items panelists estimated the proportion of minimally competent students they believed would get the item correct (Modified Angoff Method). Panelists used five-point percentage ranges to provide their first estimates (e.g., 0%, 5%, 10%, 15%...100%) in the first round. They used single-point percentages to cover the full range from 0% to 100% in the second round. For the open-response items with four or fewer total score points panelists estimated the mean score that they expected the minimally competent student to earn (item mean estimation) on the item. For the long-writing tasks with a six-point rubric, panelists were given a set of 12 student papers, selected in advance, to represent clear examples of each of the six score points; two papers were selected to represent each score point. The panelists were asked to select two student papers from the set of 12 that they believed represented the work of the minimally competent student. (Panelists did not know the scores for the papers when they made their first paper selections.) For the second round, panelists again selected the two papers they believed best represented the work of the minimally competent student.

Actual achievement data from the 2006 test takers were shared with the panelists between their first and second rounds, as well as information about the cut-scores generated by the panelists during the first round. Summary statistics were provided for the panels' first-round results including the mean, median, minimum, maximum, standard deviation, 75th and 25th percentile range of the initial cut-scores. Information was provided about the proportion of students who answered each multiple-choice item correctly, the panelist's individual rating for each item and their fellow panelists' mean rating for each item. For open-response items the panelists were provided with the mean score for actual test takers on each item, their individual mean item performance estimates and the mean of the mean item estimates across all panelists. Panelists were also shown a score distribution across the possible rubric score values. For the long-writing prompt they were also shown the actual scores for the set of papers from which they had made their paper selection decisions.

A preliminary total score distribution from the 2006 OSSLT was shown to the panelists, and they were informed of the percentage of students who would be successful and unsuccessful if their first-round results were used as the passing score. As well, prior to the second round, the panelists were informed about the rates of success for the previous three years of the OSSLT. The panelists' second-round cut-scores were used to calculate the recommended cut-score for students to be successful on the 2006 OSSLT.

At the conclusion of the session the panelists completed an evaluation form that sought information about the success of various components of the session (e.g., orientation, practice session, rating rounds, feedback), as well as their degree of confidence in the results of the standard alignment activity.

■ ■ ■ ■ ■

Over the years, EQAO has conducted standard-setting activities for the Primary, Junior and Grade 9 assessments using the Modified Angoff, Bookmark and Body of Work methods. The purpose of these activities, which were undertaken as part of EQAO's internal review and monitoring process, was to explore the usefulness of various approaches and to determine if the current cut-scores were still appropriate. Generally, these studies have shown that all three standard-setting methods can be used successfully with EQAO's assessments, and some minor adjustments to cut-scores have also resulted from these activities.

SUMMARY

This chapter explains the importance of setting clear and fair performance standards regardless of whether the large-scale assessment is relatively high- or low-stakes. Given the importance of accurate and consistent classification of student performance, and since the setting of performance standards includes subjective elements, it is important that standard setting activities are conducted according to professional guidelines, many of which are outlined here.

In conducting standard-setting activities it is critical that the foundations are solid. The composition of the panel and the method of conducting the activity are early key considerations. It is also crucial that the person(s) conducting the standard-setting session is experienced in the method to be used, and the orientation, training, materials and process must be well thought out and organized.

Standard setting is an essential activity to be conducted at the outset of a large-scale assessment program to ensure examinees are properly classified as to their performances. It is also important to consider conducting standard-setting activities periodically, perhaps every five years or so, to correct for any potential drift away from the original standards. Between standard-setting activities, statistical equating methodologies (described in Chapter 8) are used to keep the standards the same from one year to the next, even though the forms of the test will vary slightly over time. Furthermore, one of the facts of life in education is that there are periodic changes to curriculum. Whenever significant changes occur, it is necessary to establish new standards.

CHAPTER EIGHT

DATA INTEGRITY, ANALYSIS AND EQUATING

ETHICAL CONSIDERATIONS

Data Integrity

Beyond the wide array of measures for ensuring the technical quality and fairness of assessments, it is important for organizations undertaking the large-scale assessment of student achievement to attend to the processes and measures for ensuring the integrity of reported outcomes. The higher the stakes, the more important the measures and associated proofs become. "Integrity" of assessment results refers to the confidence that one can have that the results ascribed to an individual or group do indeed belong to that individual or group and have been accurately computed.

This definition implies the two main perspectives from which to consider the quality of data integrity:

- Accuracy in linking outcomes to students and in aggregating results to the groups/schools/districts to which students belong
- Accuracy in data processing (i.e., that the rules for scoring and processing student item scores into summary student and aggregate outcomes have been accurately applied)

Accuracy in Linking Outcomes

Even in sample assessments, in order for assessment results to be useful to stakeholders, it is vital that all of an assessment's components (test materials, questionnaire responses) can be reliably linked to individuals and, often, to the background contextual information about those individuals (e.g., gender, special education needs status, provision of test accommodations). EQAO invests considerable planning and operational time in assuring reliable linkages between assessment participants and their materials.

In Ontario, the Ministry of Education assigns unique identifying numbers to schools, districts and schools (Ministry-assigned identifiers [Midents]) and to students (Ontario Education Numbers [OENs]). EQAO uses these school and district identifiers to link teacher and principal questionnaire results to schools and districts for reporting aggregate questionnaire results. This is typically achieved via a database housing the Mident of the school and district to which the educator belongs and a digitally readable bar-coded material identification number assigned to assessment materials by EQAO.

In the case of individual students, accuracy in linking is all the more important, as each student receives an individual report of their EQAO assessment results along with some background information (e.g., the students' special identifications status and whether the school requested testing accommodations on the student's behalf). EQAO developed a Web application for the collection of student information from districts and schools (Student Data Collection [SDC] system). Prior to each assessment administration, the school district uses the SDC system to provide information on all students in the target population (e.g., OEN, gender, date of birth, special education needs identification, English language learner status, testing accommodations). The sharing of information is typically done via the upload of an Excel spreadsheet or XML file, with field definitions as set out in requirements documentation (e.g., variable names, types, values). EQAO collates that student information into reports for schools. Between the initial district upload and the printing and distribution of assessment materials, schools use the SDC system to verify student information, to add or delete students when they move or change schools and to indicate any special test formats (e.g., Braille, audio, large print). Consequently, the student-level data in EQAO's database is often more current that even those in the school districts' student information systems. Schools also verify student information one final time prior to the publication of aggregated results during the process after scoring when preliminary student results are shared with schools via the Web reporting Preliminary Student Summary (PSS) process. EQAO will make changes to individual student data at any time there is notification from a school (e.g., receipt of missing assessment materials; change in special education needs status), re-compute individual assessment results and reprint student reports based on the updated information, as required.

Accuracy in Data Processing

Collating individual item scores into a single outcome for each student and aggregating results for groups of students into school and district summaries requires an extensive set of scoring rules and data processing steps. It is best business practice for these rules and steps to be clearly defined and documented and accessible to all individuals whose work contributes to the shared responsibility of arriving at final outcomes. Below is a list of measures that EQAO uses to bring the greatest degree of confidence to computed achievement outcomes:

- Documentation of scoring rules (scoring here refers to how item scores are treated)
    - Explicit identification of how blank questions are treated
    - Explicit definition of treatment of unscorable student work (e.g., "off topic")
    - Defined process for handling exceptional cases, such as pro-rating student scores due to mis-printed assessment materials)
- Documentation of psychometric analysis steps, outputs and decisions
- Replication of psychometric analysis (e.g., computation and comparison) by external psychometric experts
- Documentation of computation of summary outcomes (e.g., cut-scores, thresholds for attributing absence)
- Replication of summary outcomes (e.g., computation and comparison) by internal and external data analysts/programmers
- Documentation of rules for protection of personal information (e.g., suppression of aggregated results when there are so few students in a group that individuals might be identifiable) and special cases (e.g., collusion)
- "Reasonableness" checks for computed outcomes
- Automated checks for mapping of outcomes into reports
- Maintenance of lists of test cases for rules related to protecting personal information and special cases

The principles of data integrity follow the process through each subsequent stage of data analysis, equating and reporting.

Equating and Comparability

Fairness in large-scale assessment, particularly high-stakes testing and when the results of one year will be compared to the next, also requires that the scores generated are comparable across years. Most large-scale assessment programs use the same blueprints to develop parallel tests over time. However, regardless of the rigor that goes into item and test development it is highly unlikely the tests will be perfectly comparable, since the test items and their levels of difficulty will always vary to some degree. Equating procedures are applied to address the issue of test comparability and to ensure fairness to students. Holland and Dorans (2006) state that

> Test equating is a necessary part of any testing program that continually produces new test forms and for which the uses of these tests require the meaning of the score scale be maintained over time....test equating is necessary to be fair to examinees taking different test forms and to provide score users with scores that mean the same thing, regardless of the tests taken. (p. 193)

EQUATING DESIGNS

There are three commonly used equating designs in large-scale assessment: the single-group, random-groups and common-item non-equivalent-groups designs:

- Single-group design (each form is administered to one group of students)
- Random-groups design (alternate forms of an assessment are systematically handed out and administered to alternate students [random samples] using a spiraling procedure)
- Non-equivalent-groups design (a common set of items is administered to different groups of students, either as a block of items embedded in or separate from the operational test or embedded in different locations within each form) (Schumacker, 2010)

For assessment programs that require new test forms each year, there are practical issues such as the amount of testing time and security of test items with the single-group and random-groups designs. For assessment programs reporting achievement results over time, the non-equivalent-groups design is the most practical. With this design, small numbers of field-test items can be embedded in operational forms of a test and then used as operational items in the following year's test administration. Thus, student performance on the same set of items can be compared over time using this set of common items as the anchor items for equating. The same holds true if field-test items are administered as a block either during or separate from the operational administrations in two time periods. The equating block of items may be kept constant over several years or modified slightly from year to year by replacing items with field-test items.

STATISTICAL APPROACHES TO EQUATING

The statistical equating procedures used in different jurisdictions cover a wide range of approaches. Generally, test equating relies on either Classical Test Theory (CTT) or Item Response Theory (IRT).

Best Practices in Equating

Regardless of the equating design, CTT or IRT model and equating procedure used, there are certain best practices that should be followed to ensure equating can meet the highest standards of quality (Holland & Dorans, 2006):

- The tests should measure the same construct; using the same blueprint and specifications will contribute to this.
- The tests should be kept secure and should follow standardized administration procedures.
- The student sample for equating should be representative of the population of test takers.
- The tests being equated should be equally reliable.

Classical Test Theory Approaches

According to Holland and Dorans (2006), the classical approaches to equating include:

- mean equating (the means or average scores of two tests are compared, and the distribution of scores is adjusted accordingly);

- linear equating (the scores on two test forms are adjusted to have the same mean and standard deviation) and
- equipercentile equating (the scores on one test form have equivalent percentiles to scores on a second test form).

Two examples of the application of the CTT approach to equating follow.

In the 1980's, British Columbia's (B.C.) Grade 12 exit examination program relied on distribution equating. Once the provincial results for the examinations were calculated, the distribution of scores on the examinations (including the mean scores and the percentage of students at each letter grade) were compared to the distribution of the schools' teacher-awarded scores[3] across the province, as well as provincial examination scores from previous years. The distribution of the examination scores were adjusted after factoring in the distribution of teacher-awarded scores and the scores of previous administrations of the tests. This is one of the simplest kinds of adjustments that can be made; however, although relatively easy to do, this approach does not recognize changes in student ability as measured by the test.[4]

For Alberta's diploma examinations and achievement tests at Grades 3, 6 and 9, equipercentile equating with smoothing is used (smoothing is a statistical method to reduce random equating error). In this approach, a set of items, called anchor items or common items, are embedded in two test forms that are administered in two consecutive years. The performance of the two groups of students on the common anchor items and on the unique items is compared. For example, if the mean and standard deviation of the common items are essentially the same between the two years, then any differences in student achievement on the remaining test items are attributed to differences in item difficulties and not to differences between the

---

[3] *At that time, a student's final score on an exit examination was calculated by combining the teacher-awarded mark (worth 50%) with the provincial examination mark (worth 50%).*

[4] *It should be noted that for many years, B.C. has used an IRT approach to equating and no longer uses distribution equating for the Grade 12 exit examination program.*

populations of students. In this case, equipercentile equating with smoothing is conducted to equate the two score distributions. The results from equipercentile equating with smoothing are compared with the results of the other equating methods included in Common Item Program for Equating (CIPE), the program used to complete the equipercentile with smoothing (Kolen & Brennan, 1995), to ensure that the equipercentile results are reasonable and, therefore, reportable.

To date, based on the comparison of the results from these different equating procedures, as well as on an empirical study comparing IRT true score equating versus equipercentile equating with smoothing, equipercentile equating with smoothing appears to be the most appropriate for Alberta's context and therefore is used as a major equating procedure for both the province's diploma examinations and achievement tests. An equating table is generated, which is used to adjust student scores for diploma examinations and the cut-scores for standards used with the achievement tests. Unlike mean equating, which assumes a constant difference between pairs of scores, the numerical adjustments resulting from equipercentile equating are not uniform across the range of scores and reflect actual differences in test difficulty. In this way, fairness to students is better ensured (Alberta Education, 2008).

Item Response Theory Approaches

IRT equating methods take the following item parameters into consideration:

- Item difficulty (the higher the difficulty the harder the item)
- Item discrimination (the degree to which an item distinguishes between high- and low-performing students)
- Guessing (the probability that a low-performing student will answer a relatively difficult multiple-choice item correctly)

There are three main IRT models that differ in terms of the number of parameters that they take into account. The Rasch or one parameter (1PL) model uses only one parameter (item difficulty) to estimate student achievement; the 2PL model uses two parameters (item difficulty and item discrimination) to estimate student achievement; and the 3PL model uses all three parameters (item difficulty, item discrimination and the guessing factor) to estimate student achievement (Kozlow, 2007).

Generally, before equating can begin, the items need to be calibrated. However, there is no consensus in the literature regarding which one of these three IRT models is the best to use for calibration. Some psychometricians make their choices on the basis of their philosophy, and they are committed to their chosen model. Others are influenced more by the practicalities of the situation in which the model is to be used. For instance, the Rasch is a simpler model and requires smaller student samples than the other IRT approaches. However, there are goodness of fit indices that can be used to evaluate the fit of the model to the achievement data to be analyzed, with the model that best fits being the one chosen (Kolen and Brennan, 2004; Kozlow, 2007). According to Xie (2007) the most common commercially available software programs for the two-and three-parameter IRT models are BILOG (Mislevy & Bock, 1990), MULTILOG (Thissen, 1991) and PARSCALE (Muraki & Bock, 1997).

In 2006, EQAO conducted goodness of fit analyses with various commonly used IRT models and the agency's 2006 student achievement data sets to explore alternative models to be used for calibration. The results of the study confirmed that the IRT models used by EQAO were the most appropriate for calibrating the data generated by the assessments (Xie, 2007).

Sometimes, the need to make changes to the test (because of curriculum change, for example) makes it difficult to meet equating requirements, particularly the need to maintain the same construct from one test administration to the next. When changes are made to the construct to be assessed or to the tests to be used, somewhat weaker concordances (statistical calibration or moderation) may be the best approaches that can be used to link test results given the circumstances (Holland & Dorans, 2006).

THE EQAO APPROACH TO EQUATING

One of the principal purposes of EQAO assessments is to provide evidence of changes in student achievement over time. As a result, the agency uses equating to ensure that the change from one year to the next is not attributable to differences between the difficulties of the two tests used in two consecutive years for each assessment.

The design used is a common-items, non-equivalent groups design. All of the students in a grade are assessed in one year, and all the students in the same grade are tested the following year. As mentioned in Chapter 4, the agency field tests all of its items except for long-writing prompts in one year, and the best items are moved forward to form the operational test the following year. As a result, there are common items that appear in year one as field-test items and in the second year as operational items. The students' scores are determined only from the operational items; the embedded field-test items do not contribute to the students' scores.

The modified 2PL model is used for the Primary, Junior and Grade 9 assessments to calibrate the multiple-choice items, and the generalized partial credit model is used to calibrate the open-response items. The guessing parameter is fixed at 0.20 for multiple-choice items. For the OSSLT, a modified Rasch model is used to calibrate the multiple-choice items, and the partial credit model is used to calibrate the open-response items. The item discrimination parameter is fixed at 0.588, and the guessing parameter is fixed at 0.20 for multiple-choice items.

The forward-fixed parameter common-item approach is used to equate the current year's assessments with the previous year's assessments. The equating process involves using the common items to place the students' scores from both years onto a common scale. To do this

- operational items in the current year's test are calibrated to obtain item parameter estimates;
- these parameter estimates are fixed on the field-test items in the previous year, and the operational items for the previous year are

concurrently calibrated with these field-test items, which provides parameter estimates for these operational items that are on the same scale as those for the current year;

- the recalibrated parameters of the operational items from the previous year are used to re-score the equating sample of the previous year, thus placing the student scores from the previous year onto the same scale as the student scores for the current year;
- the percentage of students at each performance level for the equating sample in the previous year is calculated from the performance levels assigned in that year;
- these percentages are then used to identify the cut-points on the common scale and
- the cut-points are then applied to the scores of students in the current year to determine the percentage of students at each performance level.

These equating procedures control for the small differences in difficulty between the tests that may occur from one year to the next and thereby ensures fairness, so that no students are either advantaged or disadvantaged by the year in which they take the test and ensures that results are comparable from year to year.

According to Pang and Xie (2008), IRT equating procedures include concurrent, fixed common item parameters (FCIP), and linear transformation of IRT such as mean/mean (M/M, Loyd and Hoover, 1980), mean/sigma (M/S, Marco, 1977) and test characteristic curve (TCC, Stocking and Lord, 1983). EQAO has examined the effectiveness of these equating models in keeping with the concept of always striving to remain at the forefront of best practices in all large-scale assessment processes. A study conducted by Pang, Madera, Radwan and Zhang (2010) concludes that the current procedures EQAO uses for equating are reasonable and appropriate and are at least as effective, or better than, other equating approaches.

SUMMARY

In large-scale assessment, it is important that processes for ensuring the integrity of reported outcomes are well-documented and institutionalized. In addition, careful, accurate equating procedures need to be applied whenever direct links or comparisons are made between the scores on one test to another. By paying careful attention to equating, aggregate results can be compared across years. Furthermore, fairness to students will be realized; this is particularly important where high-stakes assessments are involved. Implementing best-of-class procedures and paying close attention to quality in every phase of testing is crucial. However, after the test has been developed and scored, and the results are publicly released, it is often the results and how they were derived that receive the greatest scrutiny. All of the efforts that have gone into the creation of a first-class test can be negated by an error in equating. As Holland and Dorans (2006) state:

> The credibility of testing organizations has been called into question over test equating problems, in ways that rarely occur when, for example, flawed test questions are discovered in operational tests. (p. 193)

CHAPTER NINE

REPORTING AND USE OF DATA/RESULTS

ETHICAL CONSIDERATIONS

The results that are generated from a large-scale assessment should be reported in ways that are consistent with the purposes of the assessment program, and they must be understandable for their intended audiences. The *Principles for Fair Student Assessment Practices for Education in Canada* (1993) makes the following two points about reporting:

> Ensure reports and explanations of results are consistent with the purpose(s) of the assessment, the intended uses of the results and the planned access to the results.
>
> Provide reports and explanations of results that can be readily understood by the intended audience(s). If necessary, employ multiple reports designed for different audiences. (p. 19)

Large-scale assessment purposes can be many and varied. Earlier, in Chapter 2, the following list of some possible purposes was provided:

- Provide information for public accountability of the education system at the school, school board, province/state and/or national levels
- Provide information for school and school board improvement planning
- Provide diagnostic information to improve individual student learning
- Examine the extent to which the mandated curriculum is being taught
- Influence classroom curriculum and instruction
- Certify that students have acquired certain levels of competency for promotion or graduation
- Provide information for comparative purposes (schools, school boards, provinces/states, countries) over time

Examination of this list indicates that when developing a reporting system, attention needs to be paid to the level of the reporting, the content and nature of reports, the interpretive framework, the timing of reports and the audience for which the reports are to be provided.

LEVEL OF REPORTING

Results of large-scale assessments can be reported at various levels. They may be provided at the individual student level if one of the purposes is to provide information to improve student learning; at the school level to improve instruction; at the school board level to allow the central office to know how the schools in the school district are performing, to allocate district funds where needed and to improve instruction; and the provincial/state level to allow officials in the ministry/department of education to know how individual schools and school boards are performing, to allocate funds to districts to improve instruction and curriculum as needed.

As mentioned in Chapter 2, results reported at all of these levels will only be possible if the assessment is a census assessment, which all students are expected to take. Most state and provincial assessments use census assessments given the need to report at the student, school and school board levels. In contrast, national (e.g., NAEP in the U.S. and PCAP in Canada) and international (e.g., PISA, PIRLS, TIMSS) assessments do not report at the student, school or school board levels given the purposes of these assessments are to describe, explain and compare the performance of countries. Therefore, the national and international assessments use representative samples of students selected using probability procedures within each country.

CONTENT AND NATURE OF REPORTS

It is likely that a variety of reports will be needed given the different needs and nature of the audiences for whom the reports are intended. Reports and explanations of results should be consistent with the purpose(s) of the assessment and intended uses of the assessment results. They should be complete in their descriptions of strengths and weaknesses demonstrated by students and contain information that will assist and guide students, their parents/guardians and teachers to take relevant follow-up actions, so that strengths can be built upon and problem areas addressed. Importantly, each report should be organized and written in a way that increases the likelihood that it will be understood and used by those for whom the report is intended. Lastly, before a report is released, it should be carefully reviewed to ensure the results are correct and that, if interpretations are provided, the interpretations are sound.

INTERPRETIVE FRAMES

Large-scale assessments results can be interpreted in a norm-referenced framework or a criterion-referenced framework. Most often the criterion-referenced framework is the framework used, because it provides a progression of performance levels, so that students and their parents/guardians can understand what the students know and can to and what they do not know and cannot do; teachers can formulate appropriate instruction and learning activities; and the province can formulate curriculum and implement remedial programs for schools in which there are larger numbers of students in the lower performance categories than in the higher performance categories. Listed below are some example states/provinces/countries with the number of performance categories and the names given to them. The expected level of performance is marked with an asterisk (*).

- The Massachusetts Comprehensive Assessment System (MCAS): four ordered performance categories–Warning/Failing, Needs Improvement, Proficient* and Advanced (Massachusetts Department of Education, 2013)

- Alberta's Achievement Testing Program: three ordered performance categories–Below Acceptable Standard, Acceptable Standard* and Standard of Excellence (Alberta Education, 2013)

- The National Assessment of Educational Progress (NAEP): three ordered performance categories–Basic, Proficient* and Advanced (National Center for Education Statistics, 2013)

- The Council of Ministers of Education, Canada's (CMEC) Pan-Canadian Assessment Program (PCAP): three ordered performance categories–(Level 1, Level 2* and Level 3 (CMEC, 2011)

Test results should be reported in a timeframe that allows those receiving the results to use them effectively. For instance, if a purpose of testing is to provide information to teachers to improve student learning by altering instructional practices, then the sooner the results are in schools and classrooms the better (Cohen & Wollack, 2006). Furthermore, attention should be given to validity, particularly consequential validity, in large-scale assessment that is associated with the interpretation, reporting and use of results.

NEED TO MAINTAIN CONFIDENTIALITY

A written policy should be used to guide decisions regarding the release of student assessment results and information. Assessment information should be available to those people to whom it applies – students and their parents/guardians, and to teachers and other educational personnel obligated by profession to use the information constructively on behalf of students. In addition, assessment information might be made available to others who justify their need for the information (e.g., post-secondary institutions, potential employers, researchers). Issues of informed consent should also be addressed in this policy.

Large-scale assessment results are typically provided to students and their parents/guardians, teachers and principals. Individual student results should not be made public. Therefore, to ensure that individual students cannot be publically identified, most provinces and states have policies concerning the minimum number of students there must be in a school before its results can be publicly reported. In the U.S., Jaeger and Tucker (1997) recommended that if there are fewer than 10 students in a school, then the school results should not be publicly reported. In Alberta, student data are suppressed when the total number of students is five or fewer. In Ontario, if the number of students in a school is fewer than 10 (for achievement results) and six (for questionnaire results), the results are not reported publicly. Care must also be exercised to ensure that the number of students is greater than the minimum for reporting results for subpopulations such as race or cultural background, second language, type of special education need, second language and academic and applied programs.

APPEAL PROCESS

Situations may arise where a student and his/her parents/guardians believe the assessment results inaccurately reflect the level of performance of the student. A procedure by which they can appeal such a situation should be developed and made known to them, particularly with regard to high-stakes assessment.

TECHNICAL REPORT

It is wise to prepare an annual technical report that describes in detail the procedures followed for the assessments conducted each year. The main topics presented in this book could serve as the organization of a technical report. This report, which should be publicly available, provides a corporate record for the assessments conducted and brings an air of transparency to the assessment process.

EQAO'S APPROACH TO REPORTING

Purpose(s)

The over-arching mandate and purpose of EQAO are related to accountability and improvement. In its *2011-2012 Annual Report* (2012), the Board of Directors of EQAO state that

> EQAO's tests measure student achievement in reading, writing and mathematics in relation to Ontario curriculum expectations. The resulting data provide accountability and a gauge of quality in Ontario's publicly funded education system. By providing this important evidence about learning, EQAO acts as a catalyst for increasing the success of Ontario students.
>
> The objective and reliable results from EQAO's tests complement the information obtained from classroom and other assessments to provide students, parents, teachers and administrators with a clear and comprehensive picture of student achievement and a basis for targeted improvement planning at the individual, school, school board and provincial levels. (p. 2)

The more specific purposes of EQAO's assessments vary by the assessment program. For example, the stated purpose of the Primary, Junior and Grade 9 assessments is to assess the level at which students are meeting curriculum expectations in reading, writing and mathematics at the end of the Primary Division (Grade 3) and the Junior Division (Grade 6) and in academic and applied mathematics up to the end of Grade 9 (EQAO, 2007a; EQAO, 2007b; EQAO, 2009). The purpose of the OSSLT/TPCL, the passing of which is a graduation requirement, is to determine whether a student has the literacy (reading and writing) skills required to meet the standard for understanding reading selections and communicating in a variety of writing forms expected by *The Ontario Curriculum* across all subjects up to the end of Grade 9 (EQAO, 2007c). The agency expects that teachers, principals, school board officials, and Ministry of Education staff will use the information about student learning as an important source for improvement at the student, school, school board and provincial levels as follows:

- Teachers can use EQAO assessment data to complement student information they gather from classroom assessments to determine where students may require assistance.

- Principals can use the data as one source of information to validate existing improvement strategies and identify where additional interventions may be required.

- School boards can use EQAO achievement data to celebrate schools' successes and also help identify those that might benefit from additional support.

- Parents and students receive independent assessments of childrens' literacy and/or numeracy skills based on curriculum expectations.

- The general public, including post-secondary institutions and employers, receives information about student achievement that provides an independent assessment of the extent to which students are meeting reading, writing and mathematics curriculum standards.

- The Provincial Government receives achievement information that indicates the extent to which support mechanisms are having an effect and can support policy making.

EQAO takes its mandate and purposes very seriously and promotes accountability and improvement through provision of products and services related to reporting, outreach and research.

Reporting

The reports of EQAO are aligned with the aforementioned purposes and are provided at the student, school, school board and provincial levels, some in the public domain on EQAO's Web site (www.eqao.com) and others in the non-public domain to protect confidentiality. Information about reporting of results for the Primary, Junior and Grade 9 assessments is provided in the next section; information about OSSLT reporting comes immediately after Primary, Junior and Grade 9. This approach to organizing reporting information reflects the differences between the categories used to classify students according to their level of performance. Four achievement levels are used for the Primary, Junior and Grade 9 assessments, and a two-category scale is used for the OSSLT. Further, while the Primary, Junior and Grade 9 assessments do not directly count toward high-school graduation, successful performance on the OSSLT counts as one graduation credit.

Primary, Junior and Grade 9 Reporting

EQAO uses the four ordered achievement levels defined in *The Ontario Curriculum* to report student performance for the Primary, Junior and Grade 9 assessments. Level 3 has been established by the Provincial Government as the provincial standard.

An important EQAO principle is that the agency must account for all students at a given grade level; therefore, for all of its assessments, the agency reports results for participating students and also for the full population of students. The expectation is that all Ontario students will participate in the Primary, Junior and Grade 9 assessments. Participating students are those who actually take part in the assessment and for whom sufficient data are available to provide a result. The category "all students" for the Primary and Junior assessments includes students who attended the assessment but for whom there was not enough information to assign a Level 1, there were no data or the student was exempt (see Chapter 5). The category "all students" for the Grade 9 mathematics assessments includes students who were assigned an achievement level of Below Level 1 or who attended the assessment but for whom there were no data available; there is no exempt category for the Grade 9 assessments.

The individual student reports (ISR's), which are not publicly available, present

- the overall achievement level for each subject: reading, writing and mathematics (Primary and Junior) and mathematics (Grade 9);

- the student's performance within the achievement level (using five possible positions within each level) to indicate whether, for example, the student is approaching the next higher level of performance and

- school, school board and provincial results to provide comparative information for interpreting the individual student's achievement results.

The Junior ISR provides each student's results on the Primary assessment that was administered three years before, as long as the student participated in the Primary assessment in the province. Similarly, the Grade 9 mathematics ISR reports the student's results on the Primary and Junior mathematics assessments, provided they participated in these assessments in the province. The students are matched by using their Ontario Education Numbers (OEN) assigned to them when they first began school in Ontario.

EQAO prepares provincial, school board and school reports, which are made public (see www.eqao.com). As previously mentioned, a school's data are only publicly available if there is a minimum number of students (10 for achievement and six for questionnaires). The provincial report contains results for the province, as well as school board data; the school board report contains results for the board and province; and the school report contains results for the school, board and province. EQAO produces an array of aggregated results, including

- percent of students in each of the achievement levels for each subject (reading, writing, mathematics);
- longitudinal results showing changes in the percentages of students in each achievement category over time for each subject;
- percent meeting the provincial standard by gender, English language learners and students with special education needs for each subject;
- areas of strength within the curriculum and areas for improvement;
- student and teacher questionnaire results; principal questionnaire results for the Primary and Junior assessments (the Grade 9 assessment does not include a principal questionnaire [see Chapter 4]) and
- contextual data that are obtained from school board student information systems.

While the results for the Primary and Junior assessments are reported for the single administration of these in June of each year, the Grade 9 assessment is reported for two administrations: winter for first semester students and spring for students who are in their second semester or full-year courses. All results, however, are reported at the same time in September.

OSSLT Reporting

For the OSSLT, EQAO reports only two categories of achievement: successful and unsuccessful. As with its other assessments, EQAO reports results for all students and for participating students. Students are considered to be not participating if they have been exempted, deferred to write the test at a later year, opted to take the Ontario Secondary School Literacy Course (OSSLC) (see Chapter 10), or no data are available for the current administration of the test. Students may be exempted from taking the OSSLT if they are not working toward an Ontario Secondary School Diploma (OSSD). These students are not considered to be part of the population for which the OSSLT is intended, so they are not included in the results for all students.

The ISR's provide the following information:

- The student result: successful or unsuccessful
- The student's scale score (a successful result requires a minimum score of 300)
- The student's results on the Primary and/or Junior assessments in reading and writing for students who participated in these assessments
- Feedback to help students who were unsuccessful to improve

School, board and provincial results are reported separately for first-time eligible students and previously eligible students. Previously eligible students are those who were unsuccessful on a previous administration of the test, were deferred from a previous administration or arrived in an Ontario school in their Grade 11 or Grade 12 school year. As mentioned above, a school's data are not publicly available unless there is a minimum number of students (10 for achievement and six for questionnaires). The provincial report contains results for the province; the school board report contains results for the board and province; and the school report contains results for the school, board and province. These reports, which are available on EQAO's Web site, contain

- the percentages of students who were successful and unsuccessful;
- longitudinal results showing change in the percentages of students who were successful and unsuccessful over time;
- the percentages of students who were successful and unsuccessful by gender, English language learners and students with special education needs;
- the percentages of students with special education needs who received an accommodation and who did not receive an accommodation who were successful and unsuccessful;
- the percentages of students by type of English/ French course (academic, applied, locally developed) who were successful and unsuccessful;

- areas of strength and areas for improvement for the reading and writing skills measured and
- contextual data and student questionnaire information.

Additional Reports

In addition to the achievement reports, several other resource reports are produced and available on the EQAO Web site.

- The documents *Summary of Results and Strategies for Teachers* contain suggested strategies for improvement to assist educators in helping students develop and demonstrate their knowledge and skills in reading, writing and mathematics. Separate reports are prepared for the Primary, Junior, Grade 9 and OSSLT, and the suggestions are based on an analysis of students' performance on the current assessments, as well as over time, and on feedback from teachers who scored the assessments.

- School success stories (*Case Studies: Schools on the Journey of Learning*) contain descriptions of selected schools that have shown improvement over time, including improvement strategies they have implemented.

- Cohort study reports, which provide and discuss the results of analyses of cohorts of students as they move from Grade 3 to Grade 6 to Grade 9 for mathematics and cohorts of students as they move from Grade 3 to Grade 6 to Grade 10 for reading and writing.

Non-public Reports

In addition to their public school and school board reports, schools and school boards receive data files with individual student achievement results for all students in the school and school board that are not available publicly. School boards also receive data files with detailed results for each school, the board and the province. As well, these reports include the results for schools with fewer than 10 students for the achievement tests and six students for the questionnaires. Teachers, principals and school board officials are encouraged to use these reports to review the instruction and teaching materials they are using and to make changes as needed. School principals also have access to EQAO Reporting, an interactive Web application that allows them to work with their data to determine areas of focus for improvement and to identify higher-performing similar schools (demographically) from which they might obtain information about their strategies for success.

Date of Release

EQAO publicly releases the results of its assessments within 12 weeks of the test administration date for the OSSLT and the administration window for the Primary, Junior and Grade 9 assessments.

Technical Report

EQAO publishes a technical report in both English and French for each year, which can be found on the EQAO Web site. These technical reports provide detailed information for the Primary, Junior, and Grade 9 assessments and the literacy test at Grade 10, including the following major topics:

- Overview of the assessment programs
- Assessment design and development
- Test administration and participation
- Scoring
- Equating
- Reporting results
- Statistical and psychometric data
- Validity evidence
- Statistical appendix

For example, the chapter on scoring includes detailed descriptions of pre-range and range finding; preparation of training materials, training and certification of scoring leaders, scoring supervisors and scorers; scoring the responses to operational and field-test open-response items; procedures for handling suspected students at risk, offensive content and evidence of cheating; and maintaining scorer validity and reliability during the scoring session. The final scoring validity and inter-rater reliability values for each assessment are provided in a statistical appendix along with the score distributions and items statistics obtained using classical test theory and item response theory for each assessment. Differential item results for gender and second language learners for each assessment are also included. EQAO is the only Canadian jurisdiction that publishes a comprehensive, public, annual technical report.

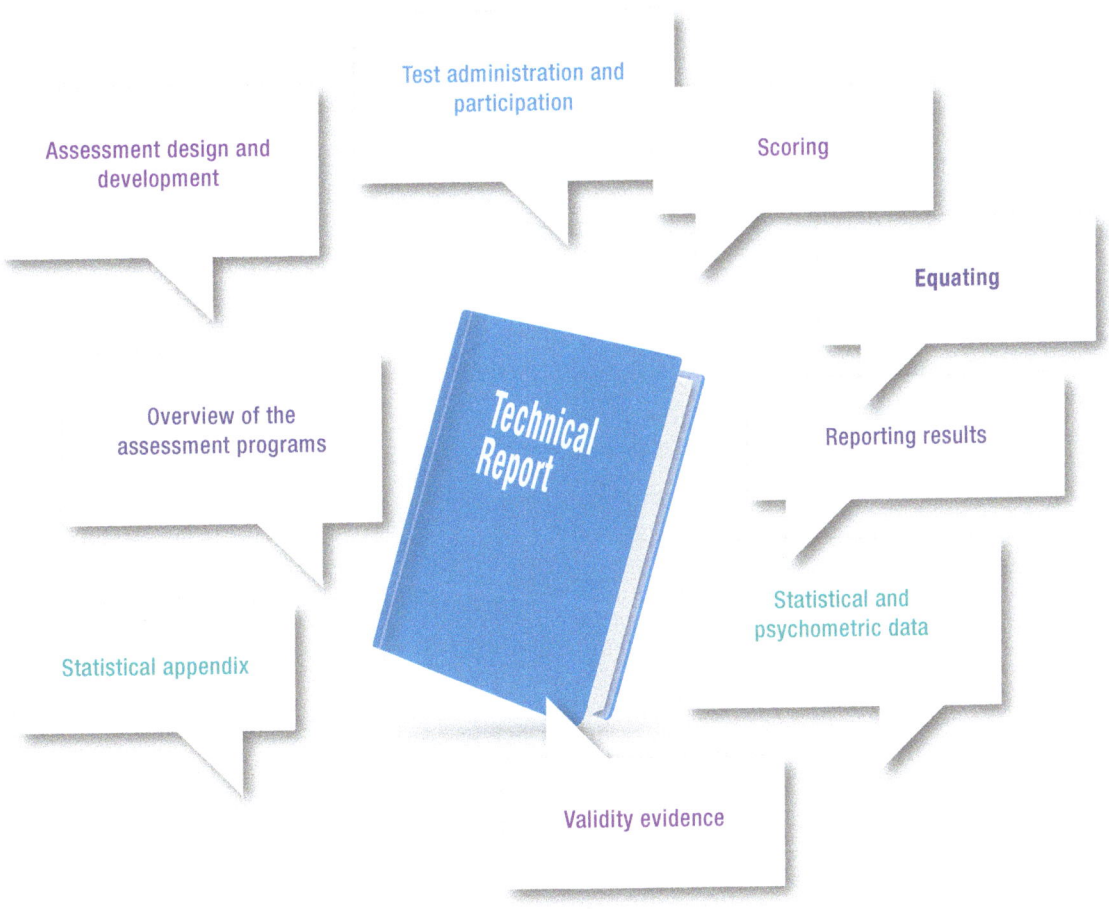

OUTREACH

"One of EQAO's key objectives is to promote the use of its data for system-wide improvement." (EQAO, 2012, p. 10) One of the priorities of the agency, therefore, is to build capacity of board officials, principals, teachers and parents to interpret and use EQAO student achievement information and results. In addition to the achievement and resource reports, EQAO has a School Support and Outreach Team comprised of approximately seven former school principals (English and French language combined). The team members organize provincial and regional conferences/forums and give presentations, information sessions and learning seminars and workshops to schools and school boards. To provide an idea of the scope and scale of their work, for the period from April 1, 2013 to March 31, 2014, the members of the School Support and Outreach Team presented to approximately 6,000 educators, 1,500 parents and 3,000 teacher/principal candidates and their university/college instructors. The team worked with representatives from more than 1,000 schools and from all 72 publicly funded school boards in the province (Lavictoire & Low, 2014). In addition, during their interaction with schools, school communities and school boards, the members of the outreach team learn a great deal about improvement strategies that work, which allows EQAO to share this important information more broadly with the field.

> Based on information gained through outreach activity, EQAO has prepared success stories from the field that allow Ontario principals and other stakeholders to learn about best practices in working with EQAO data to inform next steps for student achievement and school improvement planning (EQAO, 2013c, p. 19).

RESEARCH

The agency conducts research and develops and publishes reports and articles based on the results of its research. EQAO research projects have three main foci: trends in EQAO achievement data over time; factors that influence student learning/achievement and education quality; and statistical and psychometric processes that produce high-quality assessment data. Some example research topics are as follows:

- Cohort tracking
- Understanding gender differences in literacy achievement
- Linking EQAO assessments to 21st century skills
- Characteristics of high-performing schools
- Improvement strategies that work for schools
- Methods for analyzing and equating EQAO assessment data
- Issues of validity and reliability in assessment

Reports for EQAO's numerous research projects can be accessed on the EQAO Web site at (www.eqao.com) under the heading of "EQAO Research."

To encourage the use of EQAO's achievement and questionnaire data by researchers, the agency has made available a data portal that these researchers can access. The key objectives for the data portal are to encourage research that maximizes the potential for transforming EQAO data into useful information which can be used to leverage action and influence learning, and to reduce the time it takes for researchers to access the data. The data on this portal include the current year's assessment information, as well as data from all the previous EQAO assessments. Student and school names have been replaced with numbers so as to protect confidentiality while at the same time maintaining student and school data for the researchers to use. To obtain a password to the portal, researchers submit a short proposal in which the purpose of the research and the data needed are provided. This process allows EQAO to monitor the use of the data portal and the types of research that are conducted. EQAO is unique in providing a data portal to which researchers have easy access.

Summarizing EQAO's approach to reporting and promoting the use of results/data, Rogers (2013) states that

> Not only does EQAO report the assessment results effectively, but they also provide interpretive guides, helpful hints, videos, yearly conferences, and effective workshops throughout the school year. These make EQAO unique in Canada and represent best reporting practice. (p. 47)

SUMMARY

The keys to successful reporting of large-scale assessment results include the following:

- Matching reporting methods with the purpose(s) of the assessment (Attention to the purposes will suggest the kinds of reports, the types of information and the levels of aggregation of data that are required.)
- Determining the audience(s) of the reports (Consideration should be given to those who are interested in using the assessment results, the kind of information they need and the level of sophistication they have in assessment.)

Cohen and Wollack (2006) suggest that the reporting of assessment results is just starting to receive rigorous attention. They state that

> It is clearly essential to test validity, but most reports are usually developed without much understanding of the impact on the audience. Wainer, Hambleton, and Meara (1999) provide a methodology for development of data displays that focuses on the understanding of the test results by the intended audience. Experimental work such as this will help lead to improvements in the use of technology for reporting and will help ensure that test results are interpreted in ways that are consistent with the design of the test. (p. 382)

CHAPTER TEN

ALTERNATE ASSESSMENTS

ETHICAL CONSIDERATIONS

Alternate assessments are intended for students with special needs who are unable to participate (even with accommodations) in the assessment as delivered. As stated in the *Principles for Fair Student Assessment Practices for Education in Canada* (1993),

> When feasible, make available appropriately modified forms of assessment methods for students with special needs or whose proficiency in the original language of administration is inadequate to respond in the anticipated manner. (p. 16)

Ferrara and DeMauro (2006) explain that alternate assessments are designed to assess academic and other skills acquired by the very small percentage of students who have severe cognitive and/or physical disabilities and who are unable to participate meaningfully in provincial/state large-scale assessments. Alternate assessments provide these students the opportunity to participate in an appropriate and meaningful way.

In the United States, the Individuals with Disabilities Education Act (IDEA) of 1997 requires that students with disabilities be included in the state-wide large-scale assessment programs, and that each state will provide an alternate form of assessment for those who are unable to take part in the "regular" assessment program. Similarly, the No Child Left Behind Act (NCLBA) of 2001 requires that all states provide alternate assessments in reading, mathematics and science in Grades 3-8 that are linked to the grade-level learning expectations/content standards (Zatta & Pullin, 2004; Ferrara & DeMauro, 2006).

APPROACHES TO ALTERNATE ASSESSMENT

Where alternate forms of assessment are used, they are usually designed to be aligned with the curriculum learning expectations/content standards that form the basis of the assessments developed for the broader population of students. The purpose(s) of the alternate assessments parallel those of the "regular" large-scale assessment, although they may not measure all of the learning expectations. Thus, a curriculum framework should be developed for the alternate assessments. A good example of such a framework is that which was developed by the Commonwealth of Massachusetts (Massachusetts Department of Education, 2013).

The most common form of alternate assessment is a student portfolio. The portfolio should include work samples, which may be

- by the student or scribed by an adult or peer, if the student has difficulty producing written work;

- photographs that clearly show images of a completed work product that is either three-dimensional, temporary in nature (for example, an exhibit or display), or is too large or fragile to include in the portfolio;

- the steps, or sequence of steps, leading to a final product in an instructional activity that cannot be included in the portfolio (for example, a student arranging a pattern or sequence of objects on a table);

- video samples that show images of the student performing the targeted skill;

- audio samples that represent the student's performance and, perhaps,

- self-evaluation in which the student's choices, decisions, and involvement before a work sample, during a work and after completion of a work sample are demonstrated.

(In the case of photographs and videos, if a student's peers are shown in an image or video, prior written consent must be obtained from their parents/guardians, or the students (if they are 18 years or older) before including photographic or video images).

SCORING ALTERNATE ASSESSMENTS

Completed portfolios should be assembled in a central scoring centre where they are evaluated by trained and qualified scorers. Scoring rubrics should be developed for each work sample together with a set of criteria in order to produce a score for each rubric. Possible criteria might include

- completeness of all portfolio materials;
- level of complexity at which the student addresses learner expectations/curriculum standards in the subject area being assessed;
- accuracy of the student's responses to questions, or of his or her performance of specific tasks;
- performance of a skill in different instructional contexts, settings, using different materials, or methods of response;

- independence demonstrated by the student in responding to questions or performing tasks and
- self-evaluation during or after each task or activity (e.g., reflection, self-correcting, goal-setting).

ONTARIO'S APPROACH TO ALTERNATE ASSESSMENT

Unlike the United States, Ontario (like the other Canadian jurisdictions) does not provide alternate assessments designed specifically for students with severe learning disabilities. The Province does, however, provide an alternate form of assessment for students who have been unable to achieve success on the high-stakes Ontario Secondary School Literacy Test (OSSLT).

In 2001, the Ontario Ministry of Education established a policy that all students who entered Grade 9 in the 2000-2001 school year, or in subsequent years, are required to meet a literacy requirement in order to graduate with an Ontario Secondary School Diploma (OSSD). Most students meet this requirement by writing the OSSLT which is administered annually in March/April. The OSSLT is based on the cross-curricular provincial curriculum learning expectations for reading and writing to the end of Grade 9. If a student is successful on the OSSLT they earn one credit. If they are unsuccessful, they may challenge future administrations of the test (Ontario Ministry of Education, 2011).

Ontario Secondary School Literacy Course

Beginning in the 2003-2004 school year, the Ontario Secondary School Literacy Course (OSSLC) was initiated to provide students who are unsuccessful on the OSSLT with instructional support to ensure they develop the reading and writing competencies they require for school and in their daily life. When first announced, the course was only available to students who had had two opportunities to write the OSSLT and had failed it at least once. In 2004 the Ministry gave school principals the discretion to allow students to enroll in the course provided they have been unsuccessful on the OSSLT at least once. Successful completion of the OSSLC earns the student the literacy credit (Ontario Ministry of Education, 2011).

The reading and writing competencies assessed by the OSSLT form the basis of the OSSLC, and the standard for a pass in the course (50% or higher) is meant to be comparable to the standard established for the OSSLT. As part of the course, students maintain a literacy portfolio of all of the reading and writing tasks that have been evaluated by the teacher, so they can monitor their improvement over the course. The students also keep a learning journal in which they set reading and writing goals for themselves and track their learning progress. Evaluations during the course count for 70% of the students' final grades; a final evaluation, in which students independently demonstrate their reading and writing skills at the end of the course, counts for 30% of the students' final grades. An achievement chart, providing four categories of reading and writing knowledge and skills and descriptions of four levels of student performance, is meant to provide teachers with a standard, province-wide method for assessing and evaluating student achievement. The students' final grades are recorded in their provincial report cards (Ontario Ministry of Education, 2003).

Adjudication Process

In 2004, Ontario's Minister of Education announced that school board Directors of Education (referred to as Superintendents in some jurisdictions) may establish Adjudication Panels at the end of each school year to provide another avenue for a select group of students to meet the literacy graduation requirement. This group includes students who would otherwise be eligible to graduate at the end of the school year, but through no fault of their own, did not have the opportunity to take either the OSSLT or the OSSLC. These students must meet at least one of the following criteria:

- The student was never able to write the test because of illness, injury or other extenuating circumstances (e.g., the student arrived in the province in the graduating year after the OSSLT administration and too late in the school year to receive the course).

- The student's school did not offer the OSSLC or make arrangements for the student to take the course in another school.
- The student enrolled in the OSSLC, but because of illness, injury or other extenuating circumstances was not able to complete the course.
- The student was receiving special education programs and services, had an Individual Education Plan documenting required accommodations, but due to unforeseen circumstances these accommodations were not available when the OSSLT was taken.

Adjudication Panels are to be comprised of at least three members who are educators with expertise in teaching and assessing students' literacy skills at the secondary-school level. It is suggested Panel members might include teachers who have taught the OSSLC, teachers who have worked with EQAO to score the OSSLT and school principals and at-risk leaders who have received training in the OSSLC.

Five pieces of student work must be submitted to the Adjudication Panel, and the work must have been completed independently by the student under the supervision of a teacher. The work must demonstrate different reading and writing skills that are called for in the OSSLT and OSSLC. One piece of work can be used to demonstrate competency in any of the following categories:

- Reading narrative text
- Reading graphic text
- Reading informational text
  (For each of the reading text types above, the original teacher-selected text, teacher-designed questions and the student's responses to the questions are to be included)
  - Writing a summary (a summary of fewer than 100 words based on a teacher-selected text of 250-300 words at an appropriate level of challenge, including the original text)

- Writing an information paragraph (one paragraph based on a topic from an assigned class activity and written for a specific audience and purpose; topic, audience and purpose to be identified)
- Writing a series of paragraphs expressing an opinion (at least three paragraphs [introduction, development and conclusion] expressing the student's opinion on a teacher-assigned topic; topic to be identified)
- Writing a news report (based on a teacher-assigned headline and picture; headline and picture to be included)

School boards are responsible for providing reports to the Ministry of Education including the number of students who apply for adjudication, the number of students who are accepted for adjudication and number of students who are successful for the literacy requirement as a result of adjudication (Ontario Ministry of Education, 2010b).

SUMMARY

The philosophical and ethical appeal of alternate assessments is undeniable; however, these forms of assessment have their challenges. For example, Zatta and Pullin (2004) identify difficulties with implementation procedures, scoring, generalizability and comparability of results, as well as validity and reliability issues associated with portfolio alternate assessments. The authors also state that although most large-scale assessments (which include alternate assessments) serve purposes of public accountability, some carry high-stakes consequences for students. Jurisdictions must therefore pay careful attention to the following elements:

- Who should participate in alternate assessments? (Consistent guidelines are required.)
- What should be assessed? (There is a tension between the perceived need for standardization of assessments and the need to consider the curricular requirements of the relatively small proportion of students with cognitive challenges.)
- How should assessments be conducted? (It is important to ensure that any scores resulting from the assessment are accurate and reflect the associated learning expectations/standards.)

CHAPTER ELEVEN

CONCLUSION

It would take a great many pages to treat in detail the topics presented here. This handbook is meant to give the reader an appreciation of the complexity of large-scale assessment and the attention to detail that is required in designing and implementing an effective assessment program. Keeping up to date on best assessment practices and paying attention to quality at every stage of an assessment are crucial for a program's success.

There is an old Korean saying, which loosely translated says, "always get the first button right." If you don't fasten the first button on a shirt correctly, it doesn't matter what you do from that point on (save for undoing it and starting over) the shirt will never fit properly. This concept has applications to aspects of everyday life and certainly applies directly to large-scale assessment.

In large-scale assessment there are many first buttons. Ethical considerations should be the first buttons that underlie all aspects of assessment, since fairness in all its aspects to test takers is fundamental. In addition, the assessment program will not be successful unless appropriate thought has gone into the initial design and implementation of the program; this is evidenced through the development and public release of a comprehensive framework document. Hiring the best professional staff, choosing the "right" item writers and delivering quality training, selecting strong reading passages, hiring the "right" scorers and providing quality training, choosing the best equating and standard-setting methods for the given assessment program and considering audiences' needs in determining the most appropriate content and format for reporting are examples of important first buttons.

I trust this handbook is a useful introductory resource for those who have an interest in large-scale assessment and serves as a helpful starting point for those interested in pursuing these topics in greater depth.

GLOSSARY

This glossary provides brief definitions of assessment-related terms referenced in this handbook.[5]

Accommodations Supports and services (e.g., presentation formats, response formats, special settings, extra time) that provide students with special education needs the opportunity to demonstrate their competencies in the knowledge and skills being measured by the assessment. Accommodations change only the way in which the assessment is administered; they do not alter the content of the test or affect the validity or reliability of the results.

Alternate Assessments Assessments designed to assess academic and other skills acquired by the very small number of students who have severe cognitive and/or physical disabilities and, consequently, who are unable to participate meaningfully in "regular" provincial/state large-scale assessments.

Anchor (Paper) Student responses that solidly represent each of the score points/codes in a scoring rubric.

Assessment/Testing *Assessment* may be used to describe the collection of data and information using multiple methods, including tests. *Testing* may refer to the administration of a single measurement instrument or set of instruments; the two terms are used interchangeably in this handbook.

---

[5] *The definitions in this Glossary were adapted from several sources, including The NAEP Glossary of Terms (2013) and Educational Measurement, Fourth Edition (Brennan [Ed.], 2006).*

Bias	Assessments should be as fair as possible for the widest range of students. Test results should not be affected by biasing factors such as cultural background, gender or geographic location; in the case of differential item functioning (see Differential Item Functioning), when a difference is found it may be due to a problem with the item (see Impact).
Blueprint	Sometimes referred to as test specifications, a blueprint provides written information about curriculum learning expectations/content standards to be measured by a test, as well as the number and type of test items and their levels of difficulty.
Calibration (Statistical)	Estimation of the item parameters (difficulty, discrimination, and/or guessing) using Item Response Theory (IRT) or Classical Test Theory (CTT).
Calibration Papers	Student/examinee papers that are used during operational item scoring for ongoing training purposes; they represent unusual or difficult-to-score responses that may be identified during range finding or on the scoring floor as the result of issues raised by scorers.
Census Assessment	All students in the population are assessed with the possible exception of students with severe special education needs and students whose language development is not sufficient to address the test in a meaningful way.
Classical Test Theory (CTT)	A test score model in which a test or item score is modeled in terms of two additive terms: a student's true score, which is assumed to be a constant, and error of measurement, which is assumed to be a random variable.
Classical Item Statistics	Statistics such as frequencies, percentages, item difficulty (p-values) and item discrimination (point-biserial correlation, r_{pbis}) used in Classical Test Theory to calibrate items.
Cognitive Lab	A process in item development in which item writers try out items with students who respond aloud to the items and/or provide feedback on their thinking processes in responding to the items following item try-outs (see Think-Aloud Protocol and Protocol Analysis).

Collusion Analysis	Analysis of responses to multiple-choice items that identifies student response patterns that suggest the possibility of cheating among students in a school or across schools.
Construct	An abstract, often complex image, idea or theory that is developed from a number of simpler observable elements. In large-scale assessment, a construct is the variable to be measured (e.g., reading, writing, mathematics, literacy); often referred to as the domain to be measured.
Constructed-Response Item	An item in which students create a response rather than select a response (see Selected-Response Item); often referred to as an open-response item.
Correlation	A measure of the relationship between two variables; may be linear or curvilinear; the values of the correlation coefficient for two linearly related variables range from -1.00 to 1.00 (-1.00 is a perfect negative correlation; 1.00 is a perfect positive correlation; 0.00 represents no correlation).
Criterion-Referenced Interpretation	Achievement results/scores are referenced (compared) to an established criterion or definition/description of performance such as the criteria for successful performance or performance at a given category/level of achievement.
Cut-Score/Point	The minimum score required for performance for a given achievement category/level.
Deferral	A student excused, due to a legitimate reason, from taking a test until a subsequent administration of the test.
Diagnostic Assessment	Assessment conducted to provide a teacher with an understanding of a student's strengths and areas for improvement, so that instructional plans can be developed to meet the student's learning needs; at the class level, to provide a teacher with an understanding of the strengths and areas in need of improvement, so that instruction can be changed as needed to enhance student learning.
Dichotomous Items	Items that are scored using two response categories (e.g., correct/incorrect).

Differential Item Functioning (DIF)	Difference in performance between two groups of students (e.g., gender, second language learners) after controlling for ability differences; differences that are found may be due to a biased item or to impact (see Bias and Impact).
Distractor	An incorrect option included among the options of a multiple-choice item.
Distributed Scoring	Non-centralized scoring; scorers score student responses at home or, possibly, in a regional location instead of one central location; now commonly associated with image-based scoring (see Image-Based Scoring).
Drift (Scoring)	Scorers unconsciously but systematically assign higher or lower scores/codes, usually as the result of applying personal standards.
Equating	A statistical procedure used to ensure that scores on two interchangeable forms are comparable.
Equipercentile Equating	The scores on one test form have equivalent percentiles on a second interchangeable test form.
Estimation	Process by which sample data are used to estimate or predict a population value (e.g., sample mean is used to estimate population mean).
Exemption	A student exempted from participation in an assessment because the accommodations do not meet the student's needs (see Accommodations and Deferral).
Exit Examination	Large-scale assessments designed to certify that students have attained the knowledge and skills necessary to graduate from high/secondary school.
Field Test	New test items are administered to samples of students to determine how well the items perform prior to their potential use in an operational test; the field test may be a separate test for the new items and not part of an operational test, or the new items may be embedded in an operational test, with several forms, each with the same operational items but a different set of new items; performance on field-test items does not count toward a student's score.

Field Trial	Informal item try-outs, usually with purposeful samples of students, to determine if the new items elicit the expected responses.
Formative Assessment	Assessment that is ongoing during teaching and learning; feedback is provided to students to help them improve, and teachers use formative assessment information to improve teaching practices.
Framework Document	A foundation document for an assessment program that provides information about the program's guiding principles, the content of the assessment and how the information gathered will be reported and used.
Goodness of Fit	A statistic that summarizes the difference between estimated values or scores and true values or scores; a statistic that summarizes how well a statistical model fits a set of observations (e.g., how well an IRT model fits the observed scores on a test).
Guessing Parameter	The probability that a low-performing student will answer a multiple-choice item correctly by chance. Classical Test Theory corrects for guessing at the test level; Item Response Theory accounts for guessing at the item level.
Image-Based Scoring	Responses to open-response items are scanned, captured and stored on a server, and then following scorer training, responses are sent electronically to scorers to be scored (see Distributed Scoring).
Impact	DIF analyses reveal that there is a difference between two groups (e.g., males and females; second language learners and non-second language learners) on an item after controlling for ability and where the difference is not due to a problem with the item (see Bias).
Inter-Rater Reliability	A measure of scoring consistency between pairs of scorers who independently score the same student's constructed response (see Scoring Reliability).
Intra-Rater Reliability	A measure of scoring consistency of a scorer who scores the same student's constructed response a second time (see Scoring Reliability).

Item Difficulty	**Dichotomous items:** the proportion of students (p-value) who correctly answer a selected-response item (Classical Test Theory); the higher the proportion answering correctly, the less difficult the item.
	The point on the theta scale corresponding to the probability of correctly answering a selected response of 0.50 (one- and two-parameter models) or $0.50 + 1/o$, o the number of options (three-parameter model) (Item Response Theory); the higher the value, the more difficult the item.
	Polytomous items: mean response for Classical Test Theory; b value in IRT.
Item Discrimination	Items that can be answered correctly by high-performing students but not by low-performing students. The item discrimination in Classical Test Theory is the point-biserial correlation (r_{pbis}) and in Item Response Theory is the a-parameter.
Item Information Function	Item information function relates to the amount of information an item provides across the ability scale.
Item Parameters	Indices that describe the performance of an item, such as item difficulty and discrimination in Classical Test Theory and item difficulty, item discrimination and guessing in Item Response Theory.
Item Response Theory (IRT)	An item model that assumes a mathematical model for the probability a student will respond correctly to a given test item, taking item difficulty, item discrimination and/or guessing into consideration.
Jurisdiction	A government-defined geographic area such as a province, state or country.
Learning Assessment	Large-scale assessments designed to gauge the extent to which students have attained curricular learning objectives; results often used for school improvement and public accountability.
Matrix Sampling	Different samples of students take different samples of test items; mostly used for field-test items (see Field Test), although matrix sampling of items and students are used in some jurisdictions and national and international assessments.

Mean	Average score for a set of scores; calculated by adding all the scores together and dividing by the total number of scores.
Mean Equating	The means of two interchangeable tests are adjusted so that each test distribution has the same mean.
Mean/Standard Deviation Equating	The scores on two interchangeable tests are adjusted so that each test distribution has the same mean and standard deviation.
Median	The middle score in a distribution of scores; half of the scores are above and half of the scores are below the median; corresponds to the 50th percentile.
Mode	The score that occurs most often in a distribution of scores.
Modifications	Changes to test content and to performance criteria which affect the validity and reliability of the assessment results; intended for students who cannot take an assessment even with accommodations (see Alternate Assessments).
Multiple-Choice Item	A selected-response test item that consists of one or more introductory sentences followed by a list of alternatives/options that includes the correct response and several incorrect responses.
Norm-Referenced Interpretation	The score obtained on an assessment by a student is compared to all of the scores in the score distribution to determine where the student is in the distribution (e.g., if a student's score corresponds to the 67th percentile, then the student's place in the distribution is better than 67% of the students) (see Percentile and Criterion-Referenced Interpretation).
Observed Test Score	A student's observed test score obtained by adding up scores for the items in a test.
Open-Response Item	Sometimes called a written- or constructed-response item in which students create a response (see Constructed-Response Item and Selected-Response Item).
Operational Test	Items that have been field tested previously are selected to become an operational test; operational test results count toward a student's score; most, but not all, jurisdictions field test their items.

Percentile	A numerical value between zero and 100 that indicates the percentage of students that is below a particular score value (e.g., if a score of 600 is at the 90th percentile, then 90% of students are performing below 600).
Performance Level(s)	Descriptions of what students know and can do for each proficiency category (e.g., below basic, basic, proficient, advanced); also known as establishing performance standards.
p-Value	Measure of item difficulty (percentage correct) using Classical Test Theory.
Performance Item	An item that requires students to apply their knowledge and skills in the context of laboratory experiments, mathematical investigations, creation of portfolios and other types of performances.
Point-Biserial Correlation	Measure of item discrimination for dichotomously scored items in Classical Test Theory; item discrimination should be positive if the option is the correct or keyed option and should be negative if the option is not the keyed option (i.e., a distractor).
Polytomous Items	Test items that are scored using more than two response categories, most often with a scoring rubric.
Pre-Range Finding	Process used to select responses that represent the full range of codes or score points for each item or prompt to be used by the range-finding committee (see Range Finding).
Probability Sample	A sample of a student population selected using a sampling procedure (random sampling with or without stratification; cluster sampling with or without stratification) that allows inferences to be drawn from the sample to the population with known sampling errors.
Protocol Analysis	Analysis of think-aloud protocols in which common themes/responses are extracted from what was said in the think-aloud protocols (see Cognitive Lab and Think-Aloud Protocol).
Psychometrics	Field of study involving the application of statistical procedures to determine the characteristics of items and tests or assessment instruments (see Psychometrician).

Psychometrician	A person who practices the science of measurement or psychometrics in any area of testing (see Psychometrics).
Qualifying Test	A test used to certify scoring leaders, scoring supervisors and scorers; consists of a sample of student papers selected during range finding that are solid representations of student work for each of the scoring codes in a scoring rubric (see Range Finding).
Quartiles	Quartiles divide a score distribution into four equal size groups (the 25th percentile is the upper boundary of the first quartile, the 50th percentile is the upper boundary of the second quartile and the 75th percentile is the upper boundary of the third quartile).
Quartile Range	A measure of variability equal to the difference between the 75th percentile (i.e., third quartile) and 25th percentile (i.e., first quartile) in a score distribution (see Quartiles and Semi-Interquartile Range).
Range Finding	Process used to define the range of acceptable performances for each code or score point in each scoring rubric; involves the selection of anchor papers, papers to train scorers, papers for the qualifying test, calibration papers and validity papers; validity papers are scored at this time, with this score identified as the score of experts; there are two stages: pre-range finding and range finding (see Pre-Range Finding, Anchor (Paper), Training Materials, Qualifying Test, Calibration Papers and Validity Papers).
Scale Score	Student's score on a scale with a known range or mean and standard deviation (e.g., 200 – 400; mean of 50 and standard deviation of 10); facilitates interpretation across assessments if same scale scores are used for the different assessments; obtained from the student's observed score through a transformation.
Scoring Guides	Description of what students know and can do for each scoring category; usually accompanied by anchor papers which are selected during range finding to illustrate the range of responses expected for each scoring category (see Range Finding and Scoring Rubric).

Scoring Reliability	Percent exact and percent exact plus adjacent agreement between the scores provided to the same student work by a pair of independent scorers or by the same scorer to a set of papers (see Inter-Rater Reliability and Intra-Rater Reliability).
Scoring Rubric	A scoring tool used to score responses to open-response items; consists of qualitative descriptions describing what students know and can do for each of two or more categories (e.g., pass/fail; below basic, basic, proficient and advanced) and accompanied by anchor papers that illustrate each category [see Anchor (Paper)].
Scoring Validity	Percent exact and percent exact plus adjacent agreement between the scores provided by individual scorers for an open-response item and the scores provided by expert scorers (see Validity Papers).
Selected-Response Item	Test item which includes options from which students choose their answers (e.g., multiple-choice, true/false, matching).
Semi-Interquartile Range	Semi-interquartile range is a measure of dispersion equal to half the quartile range (see Quartiles and Quartile Range).
Special Provisions	Changes to the setting (e.g., separate room) and timing (extra time) of the test for students with special education needs (see Accommodations).
Special Versions	Presentation formats such as Braille, large-print, coloured paper, assistive technology (e.g., text-to-speech software) versions of an assessment (see Accommodations).
Standard Deviation	A measure of the variability of a distribution of scores (if many scores are close to the mean, then the standard deviation is relatively small; if many scores are far from the mean, then the standard deviation is relatively large).
Standardized Tests	Tests that are administered and scored under the same conditions.
Standard Setting	Procedures to determine the cut-score(s) that differentiate between performance of students in adjacent performance levels (e.g., between students at the basic level and students at the proficient level).

Summative Assessment	Assessment that is performed at the end of a program of study to assess what students have learned after completion of a specified instructional period.
Test Information Function	The sum of the item information functions (see Item Information Function); items for operational form selected to fit target test information function.
Think-Aloud Protocol	Students think aloud as they respond to a test item (concurrent protocol), or immediately after they have selected or produced an answer they describe what they did and/or give reasons for what they did (retrospective protocol).
Training Materials	Materials that ensure all scorers receive the same training, so that they will give the same student work the same score; training materials consist of scoring rubrics to be used, training papers to illustrate the performance at each level of the scoring rubric; qualifying test(s) to be used prior to beginning scoring and calibration and validity papers to be used during scoring.
Training Papers	Student papers that clarify the application of the scoring rubric to student responses; training papers are solid responses that represent given codes in a scoring rubric.
Universal Design	An approach to item and test development that allows tests to be as accessible as possible to a broad range of test-takers by using different formats, technologies and designs.
Validity Papers	Student papers that are expertly scored during range finding and are used during operational item scoring to monitor scoring accuracy (see Range Finding and Scoring Validity).
Validity (Scoring)	Validity/accuracy of scoring judged by comparing the scorers' scores with those of experts (considered the "true" scores) on the validity papers against minimum expected validity standards (see Range Finding, Validity Papers and Scoring Validity).
Vertically Moderated Standards	A set of cross-grade performance standards that reflect expected or reasonable growth across grades (see Standard Setting).

APPENDIX

This copyright covers material expressly for this volume by the editor/s as well as the compilation itself. It does not cover individual sections herein that first appeared elsewhere. Permission to reprint these has been obtained by Richard M. Jones for this edition only.

Principles for Fair Student Assessment Practices for Education in Canada

The *Principles for Fair Student Assessment Practices for Education in Canada* contains a set of principles and related guidelines generally accepted by professional organizations as indicative of fair assessment practice within the Canadian educational context. Assessments depend on professional judgment; the principles and related guidelines presented in this document identify the issues to consider in exercising this professional judgment and in striving for the fair and equitable assessment of all students.

Assessment is broadly defined in the *Principles* as the process of collecting and interpreting information that can be used (i) to inform students, and their parents/guardians where applicable, about the progress they are making toward attaining the knowledge, skills, attitudes, and behaviors to be learned or acquired, and (ii) to inform the various personnel who make educational decisions (instructional, diagnostic, placement, promotion, graduation, curriculum planning, program development, policy) about students. Principles and related guidelines are set out for both developers and users of assessments. Developers include people who construct assessment methods and people who set policies for particular assessment programs. Users include people who select and administer assessment methods, commission assessment development services, or make decisions on the basis of assessment results and findings. The roles may overlap, as when a teacher or instructor develops and administers an assessment instrument and then scores and interprets the students' responses, or when a ministry or department of education or local school system commissions the development and implementation of an assessment program and scoring services and makes decisions on the basis of the assessment results.

The *Principles for Fair Student Assessment Practices for Education in Canada* was developed by a Working Group guided by a Joint Advisory Committee. The Joint Advisory Committee included two representatives appointed by each of the following professional organizations: Canadian Education Association, Canadian School Boards Association, Canadian Association for School Administrators, Canadian Teachers' Federation, Canadian Guidance and Counselling Association, Canadian Association of School Psychologists, Canadian Council for Exceptional Children, Canadian Psychological Association, and Canadian Society for the Study of Education. In addition, the Joint Advisory Committee included a representative of the Provincial and Territorial Ministries and Departments of Education.

Financial support for the development and dissemination of the *Principles* was provided principally by the Walter and Duncan Gordon Charitable Foundation, with additional support provided by various Faculties, Institutes, and Colleges of Education and Provincial and Territorial Ministries and Departments of Education in Canada. This support is gratefully acknowledged.

The Joint Advisory Committee invites users to share their experiences in working with the *Principles* and to submit any suggestions that could be used to revise and improve the *Principles*. Comments and suggestions should be sent to the Joint Advisory Committee at the address shown below.

2

The *Principles for Fair Student Assessment Practices for Education in Canada* is not copyrighted. Reproduction and dissemination are encouraged. Please cite the *Principles* as follows:

Principles for Fair Student Assessment Practices for Education in Canada. (1993). Edmonton, Alberta: Joint Advisory Committee. (Mailing Address: Joint Advisory Committee, Centre for Research in Applied Measurement and Evaluation, 3-104 Education Building North, University of Alberta, Edmonton, Alberta, T6G 2G5).

The *Principles for Fair Student Assessment Practices for Education in Canada* is the product of a comprehensive effort to reach consensus on what constitutes sound principles to guide the fair assessment of students. The principles and their related guidelines should be considered neither exhaustive nor mandatory; however, organizations, institutions, and individual professionals who endorse them are committing themselves **to endeavor to follow their intent and spirit** so as to achieve fair and equitable assessments of students.

Organization and Use of the Principles

The principles and their related guidelines are organized in two parts. Part A is directed at assessments carried out by teachers at the elementary and secondary school levels. Part A is also applicable at the post-secondary level with some modifications, particularly with respect to whom assessment results are reported. Part B is directed at standardized assessments developed external to the classroom by commercial test publishers, provincial and territorial ministries and departments of education, and local school jurisdictions[1].

Five general principles of fair assessment practices are provided in Part A; four are provided in Part B. Each principle is followed by a series of guidelines for practice. In the case of Part A where no prior sets of standards for fair practice exist, a brief comment accompanies each guideline to help clarify and illuminate the guideline and its application.

The Joint Advisory Committee recognizes that in the field of assessment some terms are defined or used differently by different groups of people. To maintain as much consistency in terminology as possible, an attempt has been made to employ generic terms in the *Principles*.

---

[1] Boards, boroughs, counties, and school districts

A. Classroom Assessments

Part A is directed toward the development and selection of assessment methods and their use in the classroom by teachers. Based on the conceptual framework provided in the *Standards for Teacher Competence in Educational Assessment of Students* (1990), it is organized around five interrelated themes:

　　I.　Developing and Choosing Methods for Assessment
　　II.　Collecting Assessment Information
　　III.　Judging and Scoring Student Performance
　　IV.　Summarizing and Interpreting Results
　　V.　Reporting Assessment Findings

The Joint Advisory Committee acknowledges that not all of the guidelines are equally applicable in all circumstances. However, consideration of the full set of principles and guidelines within Part A should help to achieve fairness and equity for the students to be assessed.

I. Developing and Choosing Methods for Assessment

Assessment methods should be appropriate for and compatible with the purpose and context of the assessment.

Assessment method is used here to refer to the various strategies and techniques that teachers might use to acquire assessment information. These strategies and techniques include, but are not limited to, observations, text- and curriculum-embedded questions and tests, paper-and-pencil tests, oral questioning, benchmarks or reference sets, interviews, peer- and self-assessments, standardized criterion-referenced and norm-referenced tests, performance assessments, writing samples, exhibitions, portfolio assessment, and project and product assessments. Several labels have been used to describe subsets of these alternatives, with the most common being "direct assessment," "authentic assessment," "performance assessment," and "alternative assessment." However, for the purpose of the *Principles,* the term assessment method has been used to encompass all the strategies and techniques that might be used to collect information from students about their progress toward attaining the knowledge, skills, attitudes, or behaviors to be learned.

1. Assessment methods should be developed or chosen so that inferences drawn about the knowledge, skills, attitudes, and behaviors possessed by each student are valid and not open to misinterpretation.

    Validity refers to the degree to which inferences drawn from assessments results are meaningful. Therefore, development or selection of assessment methods for collecting information should be clearly linked to the purposes for which inferences and decisions are to be made. For example, to monitor the progress of students as proofreaders and editors of their own work, it is better to assign an actual writing task, to allow time and resources for editing (dictionaries, handbooks, etc.), and to observe students for evidence of proofreading and editing skill as they work than to use a test containing discrete items on usage and grammar that are relatively devoid of context.

2. Assessment methods should be clearly related to the goals and objectives of instruction, and be compatible with the instructional approaches used.

   To enhance validity, assessment methods should be in harmony with the instructional objectives to which they are referenced. Planning an assessment design at the same time as planning instruction will help integrate the two in meaningful ways. Such joint planning provides an overall perspective on the knowledge, skills, attitudes, and behaviors to be learned and assessed, and the contexts in which they will be learned and assessed.

3. When developing or choosing assessment methods, consideration should be given to the consequences of the decisions to be made in light of the obtained information.

   The outcomes of some assessments may be more critical than others. For example, misinterpretation of the level of performance on an end-of-unit test may result in incorrectly holding a student from proceeding to the next instructional unit in a continuous progress situation. In such "high-stake" situations, every effort should be made to ensure the assessment method will yield consistent and valid results. "Low-stake" situations, such as determining if a student has correctly completed an in-class assignment, can be less stringent. Low-stake assessments are often repeated during the course of a reporting period using a variety of methods. If the results are aggregated to form a summary comment or grade, the summary will have greater consistency and validity than its component elements.

4. More than one assessment method should be used to ensure comprehensive and consistent indications of student performance.

   To obtain a more complete picture or profile of a student's knowledge, skills, attitudes, or behaviors, and to discern consistent patterns and trends, more than one assessment method should be used. Student knowledge might be assessed using completion items; process or reasoning skills might be assessed by observing performance on a relevant task; evaluation skills might be assessed by reflecting upon the discussion with a student about what materials to include in a portfolio. Self-assessment may help to clarify and add meaning to the assessment of a written communication, science project, piece of artwork, or an attitude. Use of more than one method will also help minimize inconsistency brought about by different sources of measurement error (for example, poor performance because of an "off-day"; lack of agreement among items included in a test, rating scale, or questionnaire; lack of agreement among observers; instability across time).

5. Assessment methods should be suited to the backgrounds and prior experiences of students.

   Assessment methods should be free from bias brought about by student factors extraneous to the purpose of the assessment. Possible factors to consider include culture, developmental stage, ethnicity, gender, socio-economic background, language, special interests, and special needs. Students' success in answering questions on a test or in an oral quiz, for example, should not be dependent upon prior cultural knowledge, such as understanding an allusion to a cultural tradition or value, unless such knowledge falls within the content domain being assessed. All students should be given the same opportunity to display their strengths.

6. Content and language that would generally be viewed as sensitive, sexist, or offensive should be avoided.

   The vocabulary and problem situation in each test item or performance task should not favour or discriminate against any group of students. Steps should be taken to ensure that stereotyping is not condoned. Language that might be offensive to particular groups of students should be avoided. A judicious use of different roles for males and females and for minorities and the careful use of language should contribute to more effective and, therefore, fairer assessments.

7. Assessment instruments translated into a second language or transferred from another context or location should be accompanied by evidence that inferences based on these instruments are valid for the intended purpose.

Translation of an assessment instrument from one language to another is a complex and demanding task. Similarly, the adoption or modification of an instrument developed in another country is often not simple and straightforward. Care must be taken to ensure that the results from translated and imported instruments are not misinterpreted or misleading.

II. Collecting Assessment Information

Students should be provided with a sufficient opportunity to demonstrate the knowledge, skills, attitudes, or behaviors being assessed.

Assessment information can be collected in a variety of ways (observations, oral questioning, interviews, oral and written reports, paper-and-pencil tests). The guidelines, which follow, are not all equally applicable to each of these procedures.

1. Students should be told why assessment information is being collected and how this information will be used.

   Students who know the purpose of an assessment are in a position to respond in a manner that will provide information relevant to that purpose. For example, if students know that their participation in a group activity is to be used to assess cooperative skills, they can be encouraged to contribute to the activity. If students know that the purpose of an assessment is to diagnose strengths and weaknesses rather than to assign a grade, they can be encouraged to reveal weaknesses as well as strengths. If the students know that the purpose is to assign a grade, they are well advised to respond in a way that will maximize strength. This is especially true for assessment methods that allow students to make choices, such as with optional writing assignments or research projects.

2. An assessment procedure should be used under conditions suitable to its purpose and form.

   Optimum conditions should be provided for obtaining data from and information about students so as to maximize the validity and consistency of the data and information collected. Common conditions include such things as proper light and ventilation, comfortable room temperature, and freedom from distraction (e.g., movement in and out of the room, noise). Adequate workspace, sufficient materials, and adequate time limits appropriate to the purpose and form of the assessment are also necessary. For example, if the intent is to assess student participation in a small group, adequate work space should be provided for each student group, with sufficient space between subgroups so that the groups do not interfere with or otherwise influence one another and so that the teacher has the same opportunity to observe and assess each student within each group.

3. In assessments involving observations, checklists, or rating scales, the number of characteristics to be assessed at one time should be small enough and concretely described so that the observations can be made accurately.

   Student behaviors often change so rapidly that it may not be possible simultaneously to observe and record all the behavior components. In such instances, the number of components to be observed should be reduced and the components should be described as concretely as possible. One way to manage an observation is to divide the behavior into a series of components and assess each component in sequence. By limiting the number of components assessed at one time, the data and information become more focused, and time is not spent observing later behavior until prerequisite behaviors are achieved.

4. **The directions provided to students should be clear, complete, and appropriate for the ability, age and grade level of the students.**

    Lack of understanding of the assessment task may prevent maximum performance or display of the behavior called for. In the case of timed assessments, for example, teachers should describe the time limits, explain how students might distribute their time among parts for those assessment instruments with parts, and describe how students should record their responses. For a portfolio assessment, teachers should describe the criteria to be used to select the materials to be included in a portfolio, who will select these materials, and, if more than one person will be involved in the selection process, how the judgments from the different people will be combined. Where appropriate, sample material and practice should be provided to further increase the likelihood that instructions will be understood.

5. **In assessments involving selection items (e.g., true-false, multiple-choice), the directions should encourage students to answer all items without threat of penalty.**

    A correction formula is sometimes used to discourage "guessing" on selection items. The formula is intended to encourage students to omit items for which they do not know the answer rather than to "guess" the answer. Because research evidence indicates that the benefits expected from the correction are not realized, the use of the formula is discouraged. Students should be encouraged to use whatever partial knowledge they have when choosing their answers, and to answer all items.

6. **When collecting assessment information, interactions with students should be appropriate and consistent.**

    Care must be taken when collecting assessment information to treat all students fairly. For example, when oral presentations by students are assessed, questioning and probes should be distributed among the students so that all students have the same opportunity to demonstrate their knowledge. While writing a paper-and-pencil test, a student may ask to have an ambiguous item clarified, and, if warranted, the item should be explained to the entire class.

7. **Unanticipated circumstances that interfere with the collection of assessment information should be noted and recorded.**

    Events such as a fire drill, an unscheduled assembly, or insufficient materials may interfere in the way in which assessment information is collected. Such events should be recorded and subsequently considered when interpreting the information obtained.

8. **A written policy should guide decisions about the use of alternate procedures for collecting assessment information from students with special needs and students whose proficiency in the language of instruction is inadequate for them to respond in the anticipated manner.**

    It may be necessary to develop alternative assessment procedures to ensure a consistent and valid assessment of those students who, because of special needs or inadequate language, are not able to respond to an assessment method (for example, oral instead of written format, individual instead of group administered, translation into first language, providing additional time). The use of alternate procedures should be guided by a written policy developed by teachers, administrators, and other jurisdictional personnel.

III. Judging and Scoring Student Performance

Procedures for judging or scoring student performance should be appropriate for the assessment method used and be consistently applied and monitored.

Judging and scoring refers to the process of determining the quality of a student's performance, the appropriateness of an attitude or behavior, or the correctness of an answer. Results derived from judging and scoring may be expressed as written or oral comments, ratings, categorizations, letters, numbers, or as some combination of these forms.

1. Before an assessment method is used, a procedure for scoring should be prepared to guide the process of judging the quality of a performance or product, the appropriateness of an attitude or behavior, or the correctness of an answer.

    To increase consistency and validity, properly developed scoring procedures should be used. Different assessment methods require different forms of scoring. Scoring selection items (true-false, multiple-choice, matching) requires the identification of the correct or, in some instances, best answer. Guides for scoring essays might include factors such as the major points to be included in the "best answer" or models or exemplars corresponding to different levels of performance at different age levels and against which comparisons can be made. Procedures for judging other performances or products might include specification of the characteristics to be rated in performance terms and, to the extent possible, clear descriptions of the different levels of performance or quality of a product.

2. Before an assessment method is used, students should be told how their responses or the information they provide will be judged or scored.

    Informing students prior to the use of an assessment method about the scoring procedures to be followed should help ensure that similar expectations are held by both students and their teachers.

3. Care should be taken to ensure that results are not influenced by factors that are not relevant to the purpose of the assessment.

    Various types of errors occur in scoring, particularly when a degree of subjectivity is involved (e.g., marking essays, rating a performance, judging a debate). For example, if the intent of a written communication is to assess content alone, the scoring should not be influenced by stylistic factors such as vocabulary and sentence structure. Personal bias errors are indicated by a general tendency to rate all students in approximately the same way (e.g., too generously or too severely). Halo effects can occur when a rater's general impression of a student influences the rating of individual characteristics or when a previous rating influences a subsequent rating. Pooled results from two or more independent raters (teachers, other students) will generally produce a more consistent description of student performance than a result obtained from a single rater. In combining results, the personal biases of individual raters tend to cancel one another.

4. Comments formed as part of scoring should be based on the responses made by the students and presented in a way that students can understand and use them.

    Comments, in oral and written form, are provided to encourage learning and to point out correctable errors or inconsistencies in performance. In addition, comments can be used to clarify a result. Such feedback should be based on evidence pertinent to the learning outcomes being assessed.

5. Any changes made during scoring should be based upon a demonstrated problem with the initial scoring procedure. The modified procedure should then be used to rescore all previously scored responses.

    Anticipating the full range of student responses is a difficult task for several forms of assessment. There is always the danger that unanticipated responses or incidents that are relevant to the purposes of the assessment may be overlooked. Consequently, scoring should be continuously monitored for unanticipated responses and these responses should be taken into proper account.

6. An appeal process should be described to students at the beginning of each school year or course of instruction that they may use to appeal a result.

    Situations may arise where a student believes a result incorrectly reflects his/her level of performance. A procedure by which students can appeal such a situation should be developed and made known to them. This procedure might include, for example, checking for addition or other recording errors or, perhaps, judging or scoring by a second qualified person.

IV. Summarizing and Interpreting Results

Procedures for summarizing and interpreting assessment results should yield accurate and informative representations of a student's performance in relation to the goals and objectives of instruction for the reporting period.

Summarizing and interpreting results refers to the procedures used to combine assessment results in the form of summary comments and grades, which indicate both a student's level of performance and the valuing of that performance.

1. Procedures for summarizing and interpreting results for a reporting period should be guided by a written policy.

    Summary comments and grades, when interpreted, serve a variety of functions. They inform students of their progress. Parents, teachers, counsellors, and administrators use them to guide learning, determine promotion, identify students for special attention (e.g., honours, remediation), and to help students develop future plans. Comments and grades also provide a basis for reporting to other schools in the case of school transfer and, in the case of senior high school students, post-secondary institutions and prospective employers. They are more likely to serve their many functions and those functions are less likely to be confused if they are guided by a written rationale or policy sensitive to these different needs. This policy should be developed by teachers, school administrators, and other jurisdictional personnel in consultation with representatives of the audiences entitled to receive a report of summary comments and grades.

2. The way in which summary comments and grades are formulated and interpreted should be explained to students and their parents/guardians.

    Students and their parents/guardians have the "right-to-know" how student performance is summarized and interpreted. With this information, they can make constructive use of the findings and fully review the assessment procedures followed.

It should be noted that some aspects of summarizing and interpreting are based upon a teacher's best judgment of what is good or appropriate. This judgment is derived from training and experience and may be difficult to describe specifically in advance. In such circumstances, examples might be used to show how summary comments and grades were formulated and interpreted.

3. **The individual results used and the process followed in deriving summary comments and grades should be described in sufficient detail so that the meaning of a summary comment or grade is clear.**

   Summary comments and grades are best interpreted in the light of an adequate description of the results upon which they are based, the relative emphasis given to each result, and the process followed to combine the results. Many assessments conducted during a reporting period are of a formative nature. The intent of these assessments (e.g., informal observations, quizzes, text-and-curriculum embedded questions, oral questioning) is to inform decisions regarding daily learning, and to inform or otherwise refine the instructional sequence. Other assessments are of a summative nature. It is the summative assessments that should be considered when formulating and interpreting summary comments and grades for the reporting period.

4. **Combining disparate kinds of results into a single summary should be done cautiously. To the extent possible, achievement, effort, participation, and other behaviors should be graded separately.**

   A single comment or grade cannot adequately serve all functions. For example, letter grades used to summarize achievement are most meaningful when they represent only achievement. When they include other aspects of student performance such as effort, amount (as opposed to quality) of work completed, neatness, class participation, personal conduct, or punctuality, not only do they lose their meaningfulness as a measure of achievement, but they also suppress information concerning other important aspects of learning and invite inequities. Thus, to more adequately and fairly summarize the different aspects of student performance, letter grades for achievement might be complemented with alternate summary forms (e.g., checklists, written comments) suitable for summarizing results related to these other behaviors.

5. **Summary comments and grades should be based on more than one assessment result so as to ensure adequate sampling of broadly defined learning outcomes.**

   More than one or two assessments are needed to adequately assess performance in multi-facet areas such as Reading. Under-representation of such broadly defined constructs can be avoided by ensuring that the comments and grades used to summarize performance are based on multiple assessments, each referenced to a particular facet of the construct.

6. **The results used to produce summary comments and grades should be combined in a way that ensures that each result receives its intended emphasis or weight.**

   When the results of a series of assessments are combined into a summary comment, care should be taken to ensure that the actual emphasis placed on the various results matches the intended emphasis for each student.

   When numerical results are combined, attention should be paid to differences in the variability, or spread, of the different sets of results and appropriate account taken where such differences exist. If, for example, a grade is to be formed from a series of paper-and-pencil tests, and if each test is to count equally in the grade, then the variability of each set of scores must be the same.

7. **The basis for interpretation should be carefully described and justified.**

Interpretation of the information gathered for a reporting period for a student is a complex and, at times, controversial issue. Such information, whether written or numerical, will be of little interest or use if it is not interpreted against some pertinent and defensible idea of what is good and what is poor. The frame of reference used for interpretation should be in accord with the type of decision to be made. Typical frames of reference are performance in relation to pre-specified standards, performance in relation to peers, performance in relation to aptitude or expected growth, and performance in terms of the amount of improvement or amount learned. If, for example, decisions are to be made as to whether or not a student is ready to move to the next unit in an instructional sequence, interpretations based on pre-specified standards would be most relevant.

8. Interpretations of assessment results should take account of the backgrounds and learning experiences of the students.

   Assessment results should be interpreted in relation to a student's personal and social context. Among the factors to consider are age, ability, gender, language, motivation, opportunity to learn, self-esteem, socio-economic background, special interests, special needs, and "test-taking" skills. Motivation to do school tasks, language capability, or home environment can influence learning of the concepts assessed, for example. Poor reading ability, poorly developed psychomotor or manipulative skills, lack of test-taking skills, anxiety, and low self-esteem can lead to lower scores. Poor performance in an assessment may be attributable to a lack of opportunity to learn because required learning materials and supplies were not available, learning activities were not provided, or inadequate time was allowed for learning. When a student performs poorly, the possibility that one or more factors such as these might have interfered with a student's response or performance should be considered.

9. Assessment results that will be combined into summary comments and grades should be stored in a way that ensures their accuracy at the time they are summarized and interpreted.

   Comments and grades and their interpretations, formulated from a series of related assessments, can be no better than the data and information upon which they are based. Systematic data control minimizes errors which would otherwise be introduced into a student's record or information base, and provides protection of confidentiality.

10. Interpretations of assessment results should be made with due regard for limitations in the assessment methods used, problems encountered in collecting the information and judging or scoring it, and limitations in the basis used for interpretation.

    To be valid, interpretations must be based on results determined from assessment methods that are relevant and representative of the performance assessed. Administrative constraints, the presence of measurement error, and the limitations of the frames of reference used for interpretation also need to be accounted for.

V. Reporting Assessment Findings

Assessment reports should be clear, accurate, and of practical value to the audiences for whom they are intended.

1. The reporting system for a school or jurisdiction should be guided by a written policy. Elements to consider include such aspects as audiences, medium, format, content, level of detail, frequency, timing, and confidentiality.

The policy to guide the preparation of school reports (e.g., reports of separate assessments; reports for a reporting period) should be developed by teachers, school administrators, and other jurisdictional personnel in consultation with representatives of the audiences entitled to receive a report. Cooperative participation not only leads to more adequate and helpful reporting, but also increases the likelihood that the reports will be understood and used by those for whom they are intended.

2. Written and oral reports should contain a description of the goals and objectives of instruction to which the assessments are referenced.

   The goals and objectives that guided instruction should serve as the basis for reporting. A report will be limited by a number of practical considerations, but the central focus should be on the instructional objectives and the types of performance that represent achievement of these objectives.

3. Reports should be complete in their descriptions of strengths and weaknesses of students, so that strengths can be built upon and problem areas addressed.

   Reports can be incorrectly slanted towards "faults" in a student or toward giving unqualified praise. Both biases reduce the validity and utility of assessment. Accuracy in reporting strengths and weaknesses helps to reduce systematic error and is essential for stimulating and reinforcing improved performance. Reports should contain the information that will assist and guide students, their parents/guardians, and teachers to take relevant follow-up actions.

4. The reporting system should provide for conferences between teachers and parents/guardians. Whenever it is appropriate, students should participate in these conferences.

   Conferences scheduled at regular intervals and, if necessary, upon request provide parents/guardians and, when appropriate, students with an opportunity to discuss assessment procedures, clarify and elaborate their understanding of the assessment results, summary comments and grades, and reports, and, where warranted, to work with teachers to develop relevant follow-up activities or action plans.

5. An appeal process should be described to students and their parents/guardians at the beginning of each school year or course of instruction that they may use to appeal a report.

   Situations may arise where a student and his/her parents/guardian believe the summary comments and grades inaccurately reflect the level of performance of the student. A procedure by which they can appeal such a situation should be developed and made known to them (for example, in a school handbook or newsletter provided to students and their parents/guardians at the beginning of the school year).

6. Access to assessment information should be governed by a written policy that is consistent with applicable laws and with basic principles of fairness and human rights.

   A written policy, developed by teachers, administrators, and other jurisdictional personnel, should be used to guide decisions regarding the release of student assessment information. Assessment information should be available to those people to whom it applies – students and their parents/guardians, and to teachers and other educational personnel obligated by profession to use the information constructively on behalf of students. In addition, assessment information might be made available to others who justify their need for the information (e.g., post-secondary institutions, potential employers, researchers). Issues of informed consent should also be addressed in this policy.

7. Transfer of assessment information from one school to another should be guided by a written policy with stringent provisions to ensure the maintenance of confidentiality.

To make a student's transition from one school to another as smooth as possible, a clear policy should be prepared indicating the type of information to go with the student and the form in which it will be reported. Such a policy, developed by jurisdictional and ministry personnel, should ensure that the information transferred will be sent by and received by the appropriate person within the "sending" and "receiving" schools respectively.

B. Assessments Produced External to the Classroom

Part B applies to the development and use of standardized assessment methods used in student admissions, placement, certification, and educational diagnosis, and in curriculum and program evaluation. These methods are primarily developed by commercial test publishers, ministries and departments of education, and local school systems.

The principles and accompanying guidelines are organized in terms of four areas:

    I.   Developing and Selecting Methods for Assessment

    II. Collecting and Interpreting Assessment Information

    III. Informing Students Being Assessed

    IV. Implementing Mandated Assessment Programs

The first three areas of Part B are adapted from the *Code of Fair Testing Practices for Education* (1988) developed in the United States. The principles and guidelines as modified in these three sections are intended to be consistent with the *Guidelines for Educational and Psychological Testing* (1986) developed in Canada. The fourth area has been added to contain guidelines particularly pertinent for mandated educational assessment and testing programs developed and conducted at the national, provincial, and local levels.

I. Developing and Selecting Methods for Assessment

Developers of assessment methods should strive to make them as fair as possible for use with students who have different backgrounds or special needs. Developers should provide the information users need to select methods appropriate to their assessment needs.	**Users should select assessment methods that have been developed to be as fair as possible for students who have different backgrounds or special needs. Users should select methods that are appropriate for the intended purposes and suitable for the students to be assessed.**
Developers should:	**Users should:**
1. Define what the assessment method is intended to measure and how it is to be used. Describe the characteristics of the students with which the method may be used.	1. Determine the purpose(s) for assessment and the characteristics of the students to be assessed. Then select an assessment method suited to that purpose and type of student.

14

2. Warn users against common misuses of the assessment method.

2. Avoid using assessment methods for purposes not specifically recommended by the developer unless evidence is obtained to support the intended use.

3. Describe the process by which the method was developed. Include a description of the theoretical basis, rationale for selection of content and procedures, and derivation of scores.

3. Review available assessment methods for relevance of content and appropriateness of scores with reference to the intended purpose(s) and characteristics of the students to be assessed.

4. Provide evidence that the assessment method yields results that satisfy its intended purpose(s).

4. Read independent evaluations of the methods being considered. Look for evidence supporting the claims of developers with reference to the intended application of each method.

5. Investigate the performance of students with special needs and students from different backgrounds. Report evidence of the consistency and validity of the results produced by the assessment method for these groups.

5. Ascertain whether the content of the assessment method and the norm group(s) or comparison group(s) are appropriate for the students to be assessed. For assessment methods developed in other regions or countries, look for evidence that the characteristics of the norm group(s) or comparison group(s) are comparable to the characteristics of the students to be assessed.

6. Provide potential users with representative samples or complete copies of questions or tasks, directions, answer sheets, score reports, guidelines for interpretation, and manuals.

6. Examine specimen sets, samples or complete copies of assessment instruments, directions, answer sheets, score reports, guidelines for interpretation, and manuals and judge their appropriateness for the intended application.

7. Review printed assessment methods and related materials for content or language generally perceived to be sensitive, offensive, or misleading.

7. Review printed assessment methods and related materials for content or language that would offend or mislead the students to be assessed.

8.	Describe the specialized skills and training needed to administer an assessment method correctly, and the specialized knowledge to make valid interpretations of scores.	8.	Ensure that all individuals who administer the assessment method, score the responses, and interpret the results have the necessary knowledge and skills to perform these tasks (e.g., learning assistance teachers, speech and language pathologists, counsellors, school psychologists, psychologists).
9.	Limit sales of restricted assessment materials to persons who possess the necessary qualifications.	9.	Ensure access to restricted assessment materials is limited to persons with the necessary qualifications.
10.	Provide for periodic review and revision of content and norms, and, if applicable, passing or cut-off scores, and inform users.	10.	Obtain information about the appropriateness of content, the recency of norms, and, if applicable, the appropriateness of the cut-off scores for use with the students to be assessed.
11.	Provide evidence of the comparability of different forms of an instrument where the forms are intended to be interchangeable, such as parallel forms or the adaptation of an instrument for computer administration.	11.	Obtain information about the comparability of interchangeable forms, including computer adaptations.
12.	Provide evidence that an assessment method translated into a second language is valid for use with the second language. This information should be provided in the second language.	12.	Obtain evidence about the validity of the use of an assessment method translated into a second language.
13.	Advertise an assessment method in a way that states it can be used only for the purposes for which it was intended.	13.	Verify advertising claims made for an assessment method.

II. Collecting and Interpreting Assessment Information

Developers should provide information to help users administer an assessment method correctly and interpret assessment results accurately.

Users should follow directions for proper administration of an assessment method and interpretation of assessment results.

Developers should:

1. Provide clear instructions for administering the assessment method and identify the qualifications that should be held by the people who should administer the method.

2. When feasible, make available appropriately modified forms of assessment methods for students with special needs or whose proficiency in the original language of administration is inadequate to respond in the anticipated manner.

3. Provide answer keys and describe procedures for scoring when scoring is to be done by the user.

4. Provide score reports or procedures for generating score reports that describe assessment results clearly and accurately. Identify and explain possible misinterpretations of the scores yielded by the scoring system (grade-equivalents, percentile ranks, standard scores) used.

Users should:

1. Ensure that the assessment method is administered by qualified personnel or under the supervision of qualified personnel.

2. When necessary and feasible, use appropriately modified forms of assessment methods with students who have special needs or whose proficiency in the original language of administration is inadequate to respond in the anticipated manner.

    Ensure that instruments translated from one language to another are administered by persons who are proficient in the translated language.

3. Follow procedures for scoring as set out for the assessment method.

4. Interpret scores taking into account the limitations of the scoring system used. Avoid misinterpreting scores on the basis of unjustified assumptions about the scoring system (grade-equivalents, percentile ranks, standard scores) used.

5. Provide evidence of the effects on assessment results of such factors as speed, test-taking strategies, and attempts by students to present themselves favourably in their responses.

6. Warn against using published norms with students who are not part of the population from which the norm or comparison sample was selected or when the prescribed assessment method has been modified in any way.

7. Describe how passing and cut-off scores, where used, were set and provide evidence regarding rates of misclassification.

8. Provide evidence to support the use of any computer scoring or computer generated interpretations. The documentation should include the rationale for such scoring and interpretations and their comparability with the results of scoring and interpretations made by qualified judges.

---

5. Interpret scores taking into account the effects of such factors as speed, test-taking strategies, and attempts by students to present themselves favourably in their responses.

6. Interpret scores taking account of major differences between the norm group(s) or comparison group(s) and the students being assessed. Also take account of discrepancies between recommended and actual procedures and differences in familiarity with the assessment method between the norm group(s) and the students being assessed.

    Examine the need for local norms, and, if called for, develop these norms.

7. Explain how passing or cut-off scores were set and discuss the appropriateness of these scores in terms of rates of misclassification.

    Examine the need for local passing or cut-off scores and, if called for, reset these scores.

8. Ensure that any computer administration and computer interpretations of assessment results are accurate and appropriate for the intended use. If necessary, ensure that relevant information not included in computer reports is also considered.

9. Observe jurisdictional policies regarding storage of and subsequent access to the results. Ensure that computer files are not accessible to unauthorized users.

10. Ensure that all copyright and user agreements are observed.

III. Informing Students Being Assessed

Direct communication with those being assessed may come from either the developer or the user of the assessment method. In either case, the students being assessed and, where applicable, their parents/guardians should be provided with complete information presented in an understandable way.

Developers or Users should:

1. Develop materials and procedures for informing the students being assessed about the content of the assessment, types of question formats used, and appropriate strategies, if any, for responding.

2. Obtain informed consent from students or, where applicable, their parents/guardians in the case of individual assessments to be used for identification or placement purposes.

3. Provide students or, where applicable, their parents/guardians with information to help them decide whether to participate in the assessment when participation is optional.

4. Provide information to students or, where applicable, their parents/guardians of alternate assessment methods where available and applicable.

Control of results may rest with either the developer or user of the assessment method. In either case, the following steps should be followed.

Developers or Users should:

1. Provide students or, where applicable, their parents/guardians with information as to their rights to copies of instruments and completed answer forms, to reassessment, to rescoring, or to cancellation of scores and other records.

2. Inform students or, where applicable, their parents/guardians of the length of time assessment results will be kept on file and of the circumstances under which the assessment results will be released and to whom.

3. Describe the procedures that students or, where applicable, their parents/guardians may follow to register concerns about the assessment and endeavor to have problems resolved.

IV. Implementing Mandated Assessment Programs[2]

Under some circumstances, the administration of an assessment method is required by law. In such cases, the following guidelines should be added to the applicable guidelines outlined in Sections I, II, and III of Part B.

Developers or Users should:

1. Inform all persons with a stake in the assessment (administrators, teachers, students, parents/guardians) of the purpose(s) of the assessment, the uses to be made of the results, and who has access to the results.

2. Design and describe procedures for developing or choosing the methods of assessment, selecting students where sampling is used, administering the assessment materials, and scoring and summarizing student responses.

3. Interpret results in light of factors that might influence them. Important factors to consider include characteristics of the students, opportunity to learn, and comprehensiveness and representativeness of the assessment method in terms of the learning outcomes to be reported on.

4. Specify procedures for reporting, storing, controlling access to, and destroying results.

5. Ensure reports and explanations of results are consistent with the purpose(s) of the assessment, the intended uses of the results and the planned access to the results.

6. Provide reports and explanations of results that can be readily understood by the intended audience(s). If necessary, employ multiple reports designed for different audiences.

---

[2] The Joint Advisory Committee wishes to point out it has not taken a position on the value of mandated assessment and testing programs. Rather, given the presence of these programs, the intent of the guidelines presented in Section IV, when combined with applicable guidelines in the first three sections of Part B, is to help ensure fairness and equity for the students being assessed.

References

Code of Fair Testing Practices for Education. (1988). Washington, D.C.: Joint Committee on Testing Practices.

Guidelines for Educational and Psychological Testing. (1986). Ottawa, Ont.: Canadian Psychological Association.

Standards for Teacher Competence in Educational Assessment of Students. (1990). Washington, D.C.: American Federation of Teachers, National Council on Measurement in Education, and National Educational Association.

The membership of the Working Group (WG) that developed the *Principles for Fair Student Assessment Practices for Education in Canada* and of the Joint Advisory Committee that oversaw the development was as follows:

Marvin Betts	Michael Jackson	Jean Pettifor
Gary Broker	Michel Laurier (WG)	Sharon Robertson
Clement Dassa (WG)	Tom Maguire (WG)	Don Saklofske
Dick Dodds	Romulo Magsino	Marvin Simner
Tom Dunn (WG)	Linda McAlpine	Marielle Simon (WG)
Bob Gilchrist	Allan McDonald	Ross Traub (WG)
Nicholas Head	Stirling McDowell	Sue Wagner
Douglas Hodgkinson	Craig Melvin	Kim Wolff
Barbara Holmes (WG)	Kathy Oberle (WG)	Todd Rogers (Chair, Working Group and Joint Advisory Committee)
	Frank Oliva	

REFERENCES

Alberta Education. (2008). *Diploma Exams. Maintaining Consistent Standards Over Time Initiative.* Edmonton, AB: Retrieved October 24, 2008, from http://education.alberta.ca/admin/testing/diplomaexams/standards-.aspx.

Alberta Education. (2013). *Achievement Testing Results. 2012-2013 Provincial Results.* Edmonton, AB: Retrieved December 25, 2013, from http://education.alberta.ca/admin/testing/achievement-results.aspx.

American Educational Research Association, the American Psychological Association, & the National Council on Measurement in Education. (1999). *Standards for Educational and Psychological Testing.* Washington, DC: American Educational Research Association.

Aschbacher, P.E. (1989). *Writing RFPs for Assessment Programs.* Washington, DC: American Institutes for Research.

Berk, R.A. (1986). A consumer's guide to setting performance standards on criterion-referenced tests. *Review of Educational Research,* 56 (1), 137-172.

Brennan, R.L. (Ed.). (2006). *Educational Measurement, Fourth Edition.* Westport, CT: American Council on Education and Praeger Publishers.

British Columbia Ministry of Education. (2013). *E-Assessment.* Retrieved December 23, 2013 from http://www.bced.gov.bc.ca/eassessment/.

Center for Research on Evaluation, Standards, and Student Testing. (1988). *Monitoring and Improving Testing and Evaluation Innovations Project, State Level Activity, Annual Report.* Los Angeles, CA: Center for the Study of Evaluation, Graduate School of Education, University of California.

Center on Education Policy. (2008). *State High School Exit Exams: A Move Toward End-of-Course Exams.* Washington, D.C.: Author.

Cizek, G.J. (2001). *Setting Performance Standards: Concepts, Methods, and Perspectives.* Mahwah, NJ: Lawrence Erlbaum Associates.

Cizek, G.J. (2005). Adapting testing technology to serve accountability aims: The case of vertically moderated standard setting. *Applied Measurement in Education,* 18 (1), 1-9.

Cizek, G.J., & Bunch, M.B. (2007). *Standard Setting: A Guide to Establishing and Evaluating Performance Standards on Tests.* Thousand Oaks, CA: Sage Publications.

Cohen, A.S., & Wollack, J.A. (2006). In Brennan, R.L. (Ed.). *Educational Measurement, Fourth Edition* (pp. 355-386). Westport, CT: American Council on Education and Praeger Publishers.

Common Core State Standards Initiative. (2014). Retrieved March 23, 2014 from http://www.corestandards.org/.

Council of Ministers of Education, Canada. (2011). *PCAP – 2010. Report on the Pan-Canadian Assessment of Mathematics, Science and Reading.* Retrieved December 25, 2013, from http://www.cmec.ca/428/Programs-and-Initiatives/Assessment/Pan-Canadian-Assessment-Program-(PCAP)/PCAP-2010/Overview/index.html.

Council of Ministers of Education, Canada. (2013). *Education in Canada: Canada-Wide Information.* Retrieved December 7, 2013, from http://www.cmec.ca/en/.

CTB/McGraw-Hill. (2007). *New York State Testing Program 2007: English Language Arts, Grades 3-8. Technical Report.* Monterey, CA: Report prepared for the New York State Education Department.

Dorans, N.J. (1989). Two new approaches to assessing differential item functioning: Standardization and the Mantel-Haenszel method. *Applied Measurement in Education,* 2, 217-233.

Education, Audiovisual and Culture Executive Agency. (2009). *National Testing of Pupils in Europe: Objectives, Organization and Use of Results.* Retrieved December 7, 2013, from http://eacea.ec.europa.eu/education/eurydice/documents/thematic_reports/109EN.pdf.

Education Quality and Accountability Office. (2004). *Ensuring Quality Assessments: Enhancements to EQAO's Assessment Program: The Move Forward.* Toronto, ON: Queen's Printer for Ontario.

Education Quality and Accountability Office. (2007a). *Framework: Assessment of Reading, Writing and Mathematics, Primary Division (Grades 1-3).* Toronto, ON: Queen's Printer for Ontario.

Education Quality and Accountability Office. (2007b). *Framework: Assessment of Reading, Writing and Mathematics, Junior Division (Grades 4-6).* Toronto, ON: Queen's Printer for Ontario.

Education Quality and Accountability Office. (2007c). *Framework: Ontario Secondary School Literacy Test.* Toronto, ON: Queen's Printer for Ontario.

Education Quality and Accountability Office. (2009). *Framework: Grade 9 Assessment of Mathematics.* Toronto, ON: Queen's Printer for Ontario.

Education Quality and Accountability Office. (2012). *2011-2012 Annual Report.* Retrieved December 25, 2013, from http://www.eqao.com/pdf_e/12/AnnualReport 2011_2012_en.pdf.

Education Quality and Accountability Office. (2013a). *Education Quality and Accountability Office (EQAO), Request for Proposals for Modernizing Assessment Operations.* Request for Proposals No. RFP-13-003. Toronto, ON: Education Quality and Accountability Office.

Education Quality and Accountability Office. (2013b). *EQAO's Technical Report for the 2011-2012 Assessments: Assessments of Reading, Writing and Mathematics, Primary Division (Grades 1-3) and Junior Division (Grades 4-6), Grade 9 Assessment of Mathematics and Ontario Secondary School Literacy Test.* Toronto, ON: Queen's Printer for Ontario.

Education Quality and Accountability Office. (2013c). *EQAO: Ontario's Provincial Assessment Program, Its History and Influence.* Toronto, ON: Queen's Printer for Ontario.

Education Quality and Accountability Office. (2014a). *Assessments of Reading, Writing and Mathematics: Primary Division (Grades 1-3) and Junior Division (Grades 4-6), Administration Guide, Spring 2014.* Toronto, ON: Queen's Printer for Ontario.

Education Quality and Accountability Office. (2014b). *Grade 9 Assessment of Mathematics, Administration Guide, 2014.* Toronto, ON: Queen's Printer for Ontario.

Education Quality and Accountability Office. (2014c). *Ontario Secondary School Literacy Test (OSSLT), Administration Guide, March 2014.* Toronto, ON: Queen's Printer for Ontario.

Education Quality and Accountability Office. (2014d). *Assessments of Reading, Writing and Mathematics, Primary Division (Grades 1-3) and Junior Division (Grades 4-6), Guide for Accommodations, Special Provisions and Exemptions, Spring 2014, for English Language Learners and Students with Special Education Needs.* Toronto, ON: Queen's Printer for Ontario.

Education Quality and Accountability Office. (2014e). *Grade 9 Assessment of Mathematics, Guide for Accommodations and Special Provisions, 2014, for English Language Learners and Students with Special Education Needs*. Toronto, ON: Queen's Printer for Ontario.

Education Quality and Accountability Office. (2014f). *Ontario Secondary School Literacy Test (OSSLT), Guide for Accommodations, Special Provisions, Deferrals and Exemptions, March 2014, for English Language Learners and Students with Special Education Needs*. Toronto, ON: Queen's Printer for Ontario.

Ericsson, K.A., & Simon, H.A. (1993). *Protocol Analysis: Verbal Reports as Data (Revised Edition)*. Cambridge, MA: The MIT Press.

Ferrara, S., & DeMauro, G.E. (2006). Standardized Assessment of Individual Achievement in K-12. In Brennan, R.L. (Ed.). *Educational Measurement, Fourth Edition* (pp. 579-621). Westport, CT: American Council on Education and Praeger Publishers.

Florida Department of Education. (2013). *FCAT 2.0 – Florida Comprehensive Assessment Test 2.0*. Retrieved December 25, 2013, from http://www.fldoe.org/faq/default.asp?Dept=179&ID=1401#Q1401.

Fremer, J. (2011). *Caveon Audit Report*. Midvale, UT: Caveon Test Security.

Gaster, L., & Clark, C. (1995). *A Guide to Providing Alternate Formats*. West Columbia, SC: Center for Rehabilitation Technology Services (ERIC Document No. ED 405689).

Gierl, M.J., & Bolt, D.M. (2001). Illustrating the use of nonparametric regression to assess differential item and bundle functioning among multiple groups. *International Journal of Testing*, 1, 249-270.

Greaney, V., & Kellaghan, T. (2008). *Assessing National Achievement Levels in Education (Volume 1)*. The World Bank. Retrieved December 7, 2013, from http://www.uis.unesco.org/Library/Documents/assessing-national-achievement-level-education-vol1-2008-en.pdf.

Gross, L.J. (1985). Setting cutoff scores on credentialing examinations: A refinement of the Nedelsky procedure. *Evaluation & the Health Professions*, 8 (4), 469-493.

Haladyna, T.M. (1999). *Developing and Validating Multiple Choice Test Items* (2nd ed.). Mahwah, NJ: Lawrence Erlbaum Associates.

Haladyna, T.M., & Rodriguez, M.C. (2013). *Developing and Validating Test Items*. New York: Routledge.

Hambleton, R.K., & Pitoniak, M.J. (2006). Setting Performance Standards. In Brennan, R.L. (Ed.). *Educational Measurement, Fourth Edition* (pp. 433-470). Westport, CT: American Council on Education and Praeger Publishers.

Holland, P.W., & Dorans, N.J. (2006). Linking and Equating. In Brennan, R.L. (Ed.). *Educational Measurement, Fourth Edition* (pp. 187-220). Westport, CT: American Council on Education and Praeger Publishers.

Jaeger, R.M., & Tucker, C.G. (1997). *Analyzing, disaggregating, reporting, and interpreting students' achievement test results: A guide to practice for Title 1 and beyond.* Washington, DC: Council of Chief State School Officers.

Jones, R.M., & Hunter, D.M. (1996). Setting achievement standards/expectations for large-scale student assessments. *The Canadian Journal of Program Evaluation,* 11 (1), 35-61.

Klinger, D.A., DeLuca, C., & Miller, T. (2008). The evolving culture of large-scale assessments in Canadian education. *Canadian Journal of Educational Administration and Policy,* 76 (July 3), 1-17.

Kolen, M.J., & Brennan, R.L. (1995). *Test Equating Methods and Practices.* New York: Springer-Verlag.

Kolen, M.J., & Brennan, R.L. (2004). *Test Equating, Scaling, and Linking: Methods and Practices, 2nd Edition.* New York: Springer-Verlag.

Kozlow, M. (2007). *Model Selection for the Analysis of EQAO Assessment Data.* Toronto, ON: Education Quality and Accountability Office.

Lavictoire, F., & Low, M. (2014). *School Support and Outreach Initiatives 2014-2015 and Summary of 2013-2014 Activities.* Report prepared for EQAO's Board of Directors, August 21, 2014.

Legislative Assembly of Ontario. (1996). *Education Quality and Accountability Office Act.* Retrieved March 30, 2014, from http://www.e-laws.gov.on.ca/html/statutes/english/elaws_statutes_96e11_e.htm.

Lin, J. (2006). The bookmark procedure for setting cut-scores and finalizing performance standards: strengths and weaknesses. *The Alberta Journal of Educational Research,* 52 (1), Spring 2006, 36-52.

Loyd, B.H., & Hoover, H.D. (1980). Vertical equating using the Rasch Model. *Journal of Educational Measurement,* 17, 179-193.

Mantel, N., & Haenszel, W. (1959). Statistical aspects of the analysis of data from retrospective studies of disease. *Journal of the National Cancer Institute, 22*, 719-748.

Mantel, N. (1963). Chi-square tests with one degree of freedom: Extensions of the Mantel-Haenszel procedure. *Journal of the American Statistical Association, 58*, 690-700.

Marco, G.L. (1977). Item characteristic curve solutions to three intractable testing problems. *Journal of Educational Measurement, 14*, 139-160.

Massachusetts Department of Education. (2013). *2012 MCAS and MCAS-Alt Technical Report.* Malden, MA: Retrieved December 25, 2013, from http://www.mcas-servicecenter.com/documents/MA/Technical%20Report/2012_Tech/2011-12%20MCAS%20Tech%20Rep.pdf.

Michigan Department of Education Bureau of Assessment and Accountability, & Measurement Incorporated. (2012). *Michigan Educational Assessment Program Technical Report 2011-2012.* Retrieved December 25, 2013, from http://www.michigan.gov/documents/mde/MEAP_2010-2011_Technical_Report_394693_7.pdf.

Mislevy, R.J., & Bock, R.D. (1990). *BILOG 3: Item Analysis and Test Scoring with Binary Logistic Models.* Chicago, IL: Scientific Software International, Inc.

Muraki, E., & Bock, R.D. (1997). *PARSCALE 3: IRT Based Test Scoring and Item Analysis for Graded Items and Rating Scales.* Chicago, IL: Scientific Software International, Inc.

National Assessment of Educational Progress. (2013). *The NAEP Glossary of Terms.* Retrieved December 28, 2013, from http://nces.ed.gov/nationsreportcard/glossary.aspx.

National Center for Education Statistics. (2013). *National Assessment of Educational Progress (NAEP).* Retrieved December 25, 2013, from http://nces.ed.gov/nationsreportcard/glossary.aspx.

National Governors Association Center for Best Practices, & Council of Chief State School Officers. (2013). *Common Core State Standards.* National Governors Association Center for Best Practices, Council of Chief State School Officers, Washington, D.C. Retrieved December 8, 2013, from http://www.corestandards.org/.

Nebraska Department of Education. (2012). *State of Nebraska, Request For Proposal For Contractual Services Form, RFP#NDE-12-449-01.* Retrieved December 15, 2013, from http://www.education.ne.gov/assessment/rfp.htm.

New York State Education Department. (2013a). *Request For Proposals (RFP), RFP Proposal #13-026, Elementary, Intermediate (Middle) Level, and High School New York State English as a Second Language Achievement Test (NY SESLAT)*. Retrieved December 15, 2013, from http://www.p12.nysed.gov/compcontracts/13-026/nysed-rfp-13-026.pdf.

New York State Education Department. (2013b). *New York State Alternate Assessment (NYSAA)*. Retrieved December 27, 2013, from http://www.p12.nysed.gov/assessment/nysaa/.

Office of the Auditor General. (2009). *2009 Annual Report: Chapter 3, Education Quality and Accountability Office*. Toronto, ON: Queen's Printer for Ontario.

Olsson, U., Drasgow, F., & Dorans, N.J. (1982). The polyserial correlation coefficient. *Psychometrika*, 47, 337-347.

Ontario Ministry of Education. (2003). *The Ontario Curriculum, English: The Ontario Secondary School Literacy Course (OSSLC), Grade 12*. Toronto, ON: Queen's Printer for Ontario. Retrieved October 15, 2008, from http://www.edu.gov.on.ca/eng/curriculum/secondary/english12curr.pdf.

Ontario Ministry of Education. (2004). *Student Enrolment in the OSSLC: Guidelines for Principals*. Policy Memorandum to Principals of secondary schools from the Deputy Minister of Education.

Ontario Ministry of Education. (2007). *Graduation Literacy Requirement: Adjudication Process for 2007*. Memorandum to Student Success Leaders from the Director of the Curriculum and Assessment Policy Branch and the Director of the French-Language Education Policy and Programs Branch.

Ontario Ministry of Education. (2010a). *Growing Success: Assessment, Evaluation, and Reporting in Ontario Schools, First Edition, Covering Grades 1 to 12*. Toronto, ON: Queen's Printer for Ontario.

Ontario Ministry of Education. (2010b). *The Literacy Graduation Requirement–Adjudication Application Form*. Retrieved December 27, 2013, from http://cal2.edu.gov.on.ca/march2010/LiteracyGraduationRequirement_OSS.pdf.

Ontario Ministry of Education. (2011). *Ontario Schools, Kindergarten to Grade 12, Policy and Program Requirements*. Toronto, ON: Queen's Printer for Ontario.

Organisation for Economic Co-operation and Development. (2013). *PISA FAQ*. Retrieved December 23, 2013, from http://www.oecd.org/pisa/aboutpisa/pisafaq.htm.

Pang, X., Madera, E., Radwan, N., & Zhang, S. (2010). *A Comparison of Four Test Equating Methods*. Report prepared for the Education Quality and Accountability Office. Retrieved December 25, 2013, from http://www.eqao.com/Research/research.aspx?Lang=E#bestassessmentpractices.

Pang, X., & Xie, Y. (2008). *Assessing Different Equating Methods*. Proposal submitted to the Education Quality and Accountability Office.

Partnership for Assessment of Readiness for College and Careers. (2013). *Partnership for Assessment of Readiness for College and Careers*. Retrieved December 8, 2013, from http://www.parcconline.org/.

Partnership For 21st Century Skills. (2011). *Framework For 21st Century Learning*. Retrieved December 8, 2013, from http://www.p21.org/our-work/p21-framework.

Plake, B.S., & Hambleton, R.K. (2001). The analytic judgment method for setting standards on complex performance assessments. In G.J. Cizek (Ed.), *Setting Performance Standards: Concepts, Methods, and Perspectives* (pp. 283-312). Mahwah, NJ: Lawrence Erlbaum Associates.

Plake, B.S., Rodeck, E., & Davis, S. (2006). *Standard Alignment Activity for the 2006 OSSLT*. Final report prepared for the Education Quality and Accountability Office.

Popham, W.J. (2001). *The Truth About Testing: An Educator's Call to Action*. Alexandria, VA: Association for Supervision and Curriculum Development.

Porter-Roth, B. (2001). *Request for Proposal: A Guide to Effective RFP Development*. Reading, MA: Addison Wesley Publishing.

Principles for Fair Student Assessment Practices for Education in Canada. (1993). Edmonton, Alberta: Joint Advisory Committee. Retrieved December 21, 2013, from http://www2.education.ualberta.ca/educ/psych/crame/files/eng_prin.pdf.

Radwan, N., & Rogers, W.T. (2006). A critical analysis of the body of work method for setting cut-scores. *The Alberta Journal of Educational Research*, 52 (1), Spring 2006, 65-79.

Rakow, S.J., & Gee, T.C. (1987). Test science, not reading. *Science Teacher*, 54 (2), 28-31.

Redfield, D. (2001). *Critical Issues in Large-Scale Assessment: A Resource Guide*. Washington, DC: Council of Chief State School Officers and AEL, Inc.

Rickwood, L. (2013). School exams going high tech. *Calgary Herald*, August 27, 2013. Retrieved December 23, 2013, from http://www.calgaryherald.com/news/.

Rodriguez, M.C. (2002). Choosing an item format. In Tindal, G., & Haladyna, T.M. (Eds.). *Large-Scale Assessment Programs for All Students: Validity, Technical Adequacy, and Implementation.* Mahwah, NJ: Lawrence Erlbaum Associates, Inc.

Rogers, W.T. (2013). *What is the Quality of EQAO Assessments? Excellent!* Toronto, ON: Queen's Printer for Ontario.

Rogers, W.T., & Ricker, K.L. (2006). Establishing performance standards and setting cut-scores. *Alberta Journal of Educational Research,* 52 (1), 16-24.

Roussos, L.A., & Stout, W.F. (1996). A multidimensionality-based DIF analysis paradigm. *Applied Psychological Measurement,* 20 (4), 355-371.

Royal Commission on Learning. (1994). *For the Love of Learning: Report of the Royal Commission on Learning (Short Version).* Toronto, ON: Queen's Printer for Ontario.

Schumacker, R.E. (2010). *Test Equating.* Applied Measurement Associates. Retrieved January 1, 2014, from http://www.appliedmeasurementassociates.com/ama/assets/File/TEST%2520EQUATING.pdf.

Smarter Balanced Assessment Consortium. (2013). *Smarter Balanced Assessment Consortium.* Retrieved December 8, 2013, from http://www.smarterbalanced.org/.

Stocking, M.L., & Lord, F.M. (1983). Developing a common metric in item response theory. *Applied Psychological Measurement,* 7, 201-210.

Takayama, K. (2013). *National Testing in Japan and Australia: To Publish or Not to Publish Scores?* Retrieved December 7, 2013, from http://www.asiapacificmemo.ca/national-testing/.

Thissen, D. (1991). *MULTILOG: Multiple Category Item Analysis and Test Scoring Using Item Response Theory.* Chicago, IL: Scientific Software International, Inc.

Thompson, S.J., Johnstone, C.J., & Thurlow, M.L. (2002). *Universal Design Applied to Large Scale Assessments.* NCEO Synthesis Report 44. Minneapolis, MN: University of Minnesota, National Center on Educational Outcomes. Retrieved September 4, 2008, from http://education.umn.edu/NCEO/OnlinePubs/Synthesis44.html.

U.S. Department of Education, Office of the Secretary, Office of Public Affairs. (2004). *A Guide to Education and No Child Left Behind.* Washington, D.C.

Utah State Office of Education. (2012). *Utah State Office of Education, Utah Statewide Computer Adaptive Assessment System.* Retrieved December 15, 2013, from http://www.schools.utah.gov/assessment/Adaptive-Assessment-System/USCAAS-RFP.aspx.

Volante, L. (2006). An alternative vision for large-scale assessment in Canada. *Journal of Teaching and Learning,* 4, 1-14.

Wainer, H., Hambleton, R.K., & Meara, K. (1999). Alternative displays for communicating NAEP results: A redesign and validity study. *Journal of Educational Measurement,* 36, 301-335.

Wilson, R.J. (2006). *Standard Clarification for the Ontario Secondary School Literacy Test (OSSLT).* A report prepared for the Education Quality and Accountability Office.

Wolfe, R., Childs, R., & Elgie, S. (2004). *Ensuring Quality Assessments: A Project to Refine and Affirm Assessment Processes. Final Report of the External Evaluation of EQAO's Assessment Processes.* Toronto, ON: Report prepared by the Ontario Institute for Studies in Education of the University of Toronto for the Education Quality and Accountability Office.

Xie, Y. (2006). *Study of Psychometric Issues for EQAO Assessments.* Toronto, ON: Education Quality and Accountability Office.

Xie, Y. (2007). *Model Selection for Calibration of EQAO Assessments.* Toronto, ON: Education Quality and Accountability Office.

Zatta, M.C., & Pullin, D.C. (2004). Education and alternate assessment for students with significant disabilities: Implications for educators. *Education Policy Analysis Archives,* 12 (16), 1-26.

Zucker, S., Sassman, C., & Case, B.J. (2004). *Cognitive Labs – Technical Report.* San Antonio, TX: Pearson, Inc. Retrieved October 7, 2008 from http://harcourtassessment.com/NR/rdonlyres/E5CD33E6-D234-46F3-885A-9358575372FB/0/CognitiveLabs_Final.pdf.

www.ingramcontent.com/pod-product-compliance
Lightning Source LLC
Chambersburg PA
CBHW040310240426
43666CB00021B/2917